HEALING
AND
DEPRESSION

Finding Peace in the
Midst of Transition,
Turmoil, or Illness

The Spiritual Strengths Healing Plan

Richard P. Johnson, Ph.D.

ISBN 978-0-9895130-7-4

10 9 8 7 6 5 4 3 2 1

First Edition

Cover design by Megan Irwin

Edited by Maggie Singleton

Printed in the United States of America

BOOKS IN THE SPIRITUAL STRENGTHS HEALING SERIES

by Richard P. Johnson

- God Give Me Strength! Finding the Inner Power to Turn Your Illness/Brokenness/Life Transition Around

- Discover Your Spiritual Strengths: Find Health, Healing, and Happiness (flagship book of the Spiritual Strengths Healing Plan)

- Body, Mind, Spirit: Tapping the Healing Power Within

- Prayers for Spiritual Strength: Physical Illnesses, Emotional Broken Places, and/or Spiritual Dis-eases

- The Ten Most Effective Self-Care Healing Techniques: What You Can Do to Maximize Your Healing Journey

- The Power of Smiling: Using Positive Psychology for Optimal Health & Healing

- Healing Wisdom: 101 Spiritual Truths for Healing Your Illness

- Healing and Depression: Finding Peace in the Midst of Transition, Turmoil, or Illness

- Staying Spiritually Centered for Optimal Healing: Even When You're Sick or Life Seems Out of Control

- Seeking Significance: How to Discover New Self-Direction and New Life-Purpose Beyond Your (Unwanted) Life Transition

Caregiving Titles

- Caregiving from Your Spiritual Strengths: The Ten Fundamental Principles for Optimal Success

- Because I Care...Inspiration for Caregiving for Spouses, Health Care Personnel, Family & Friends

The Spiritual Strengths Healing Plan

The Spiritual Strengths Healing Plan allows you to harness your internal healing power! It is not "faith healing" in which one relies on divine intervention as the sole means for physical cure, nor does it promise cure. Its purpose is healing and is best seen as a supplement to and support for current medical practices. The Spiritual Strengths Healing Plan's philosophy holds that each individual needs to seek the best and most appropriate medical and psychological care they can, in accord with their own personal wishes, and supplement their care with this Plan.

Please note that you will see the word "illness" throughout this book in its broadest sense and may indicate any (or a combination) of the following:

I. Physical Sicknesses

Cancer, heart disease, MS, Lupus, migraine, addictions, hypochondriasis, pain, weight management/loss, smoking cessation, pneumonia, COPD, hypertension, arthritis, immune disorders, Parkinson's, diabetes, stroke, chronic fatigue etc., etc.

II. Psychological Issues

Anxiety, depression, personality disorders, OCD, manipulation, stress, bi-polar disorder, etc., etc.

III. Emotional Issues

Being unrealistic, lacking responsibility, low-self-esteem, career focus issues, poor organization skills, family disharmony, anger management, fears, perfectionism, marriage discontent, lifelessness, infidelity, irritability, chronic lateness, caregiving, etc., etc.

IV. Spiritual Dis-eases

Peace of mind and heart, un-forgiveness, existential angst, inner pain, grudges, scrupulosity, incomplete developmental transitions, guilt, grief and unresolved grief, regrets, blame, disappointments, so-called "unfinished business," resentments, etc., etc.

V. Spiritual Direction & Growth

Gaining better clarity of God's plan in your life, and breaking through barriers that may be hindering your faith journey.

Where do <u>you</u> need healing?

For more information about the Spiritual Strengths Healing Plan, log on to...

<u>www.SpiritualStrengthsHealing.com</u>

The Spiritual Strengths Healing Institute

Learning the art of healing for self and others

Contents

Introduction

This book strives to—

- Prevent you from falling into depression during your illness journey.

- Help you get out of depression if you have already experienced its effects during your illness journey.

- Keep you "feeling good" beyond your illness treatment and for the rest of your life.

After the initial shock of any diagnosis of illness, and after the anger subsides, what's left too often is some form of depression. Indeed, depression is perhaps the most common long-term emotional reaction experienced by persons with illness. Depression has many faces; there are probably as many different expressions of depression as there are people suffering from it. Some persons with illness may say, "*I feel depressed today.*" and only mean that they feel awkward, a bit down, or simply out-of-sorts. Other persons with illness mean something very different; they feel emotionally devastated and distorted. They feel something much more than simply having a "bad day."

Depression is not confined to the person with illness; it can embroider itself like an expanding net over illness caregivers, family members, friends, acquaintances, etc. as well. The tentacles of depression smother whatever they touch. Like a kudzu vine in the Deep South, depression, left unattended, eventually covers its' "prey" and re-sculpts your inner terrain into unrecognizable, surrealistic and fearsome landscapes of darkness.

9

Depression can overtake you and infect your soul—leaving you to feel like a hollow shell of your former self. Depression can rob you of you.

This book is about a new approach for dealing with whatever forms of depression might visit you (care receiver and caregiver alike) during your active involvement with illness and beyond. The fundamental uniqueness of this new approach is that it activates the internal healing mechanisms that already exist within you. The approach follows what I call a new "Law of Healing" based on the **Spiritual Strengths Healing Plan** which involves these six steps:

1. Know that you have the power to channel the healing energy (spiritual strengths), which God has invested in you through grace, onto your depression.

2. Become increasing aware of your hidden self-sabotaging, anti-grace forces (shadows and compulsions) that keep your depression active.

3. Learn effective techniques to re-program your thoughts toward healing your depression and gain better alignment with God's grace.

4. Develop a keener understanding of your feelings so you can use them as self-motivational mechanisms of grace to propel you beyond whatever ways depression may be hobbling you. This understanding will help you see past the illusionary conclusion that your feelings somehow define the real you.

5. Enlist the grand internal mechanisms of choice so you can generously exercise your free will decision-making abilities to bring about a new tomorrow.

6. Form new behaviors of health that can free you from the clutches of depression.

I've worked with and counseled literally hundreds of persons who have suffered from depression in one form or another. Each and every one of these persons, from all walks of life, benefited from the program outlined in this book. I don't possess any special or miraculous powers of healing; no, it's not me that heals. The fact is that the power of healing your depression during your illness journey is God-given, and its power is inside of you. Healing power has been in you all along; God placed it there at your conception. I've simply developed a program that lets you unleash this vital power that's been dammed-up inside of you. The Spiritual Strengths Healing Plan captures your healing power and then lets it wash over your personality with spiritual healing balm.

As I've written in Discover Your Spiritual Strengths, the flagship book of the Spiritual Strengths Healing Plan, I recognized that there were some hospital patients who seemed to withstand the intense emotional trauma of surgery and/or life-threatening illness, and didn't get depressed. I came to understand that these "spiritually-healing patients" were tapping into their own internal sacredness, the power of the divine that allowed them to transcend the emotional "junk" of illness and remain clear-headed, upbeat, positive, and even cheerful in the face of the grave consequence of their disease.

Imagery

This book is about using guided imagination to find a way to personality realignment, to discover the path back to the center of your personality where the universal healing power of God resides in your spiritual strengths. This short book then is a guidebook, a kind of map, which shows you the way to go home to your center, home to your soul, and there find peace of mind and heart. It is my hope and prayer that this book does exactly that for you.

This book can certainly stand on its own, but it is probably best used in conjunction with the Spiritual Strengths Healing Plan. Combining the efforts within this book with the resources found at www.spiritualstrengthshealing.com can propel you into a heightened and more illuminated plane where you can better see God's grace that is waiting there, poised and ready to take you to your new tomorrow beyond illness and beyond depression. To do this—

1. Discover your unique set of spiritual strengths when you take the Spiritual Strengths Healing Profile (SSHP).

2. Incorporate the Seven-Week Inner Healing Immersion Program into your healing regimen.

3. Use the personal daily prayers found in the Healing Prayers book to remain spiritually centered during this time in your life.

This book stands on the shoulders of former medical and psychological researchers who have demonstrated the vitalizing benefits of "guided imagery," or imagination, in overcoming the emotional, psychological, and spiritual "negatives" of the illness of illness.

Drs. Jeanne Achterberg and Frank Lawlis found that the ways that patients imagined their immune system working did indeed have an effect on their disease progression. Those persons with illness who formulated clearer mental pictures of their immune system experienced better treatment outcomes. In short, those who saw their immune system functioning from strength, rather than weakness, did better.

Researcher O. Carl Simonton, M.D. wrote, "*Healthy images increase your sense of power, well-being, and peace of mind. They strengthen your sense of connectedness with your inner wisdom, with others, with the world and the universe.*" (The Healing Journey, page 67-8).

Renowned neurobiologist, Dr. Blair Justice has written, "*What goes on in our heads profoundly affects what goes on in our bodies.*" (Who Gets Sick? page 16). I would add that it's not just what goes on in our head, but also what goes on in our hearts (feelings) and what goes on in our souls (connections with divinity) that also dramatically affect what goes on in our bodies. Grand new frontiers of scientific investigation have opened up—exciting new evidence that this is so.

The Spiritual Strengths Healing Plan represents a new way of removing the fangs from anger and depression before they grow ferocious and subvert the meaning and growth from your illness journey. I invite you to sit back with this book, use it as a reference and an inspiration—find new peace, understanding, and even vitality in its pages.

PLEASE NOTE: One of the essential assumptions of the Spiritual Strengths Healing Plan is that you should pursue the best care possible; this includes the best medical care, the best psychological care, and the best spiritual care. Dealing with depression many times requires medical care in the form of an antidepressant and perhaps other psychotropic medications available from your doctor. Dealing with depression may also include seeing competent mental health professionals such as psychiatrists, psychologists, professional counselors, clinical social workers, and the like. I encourage you to take advantage of these wonderful therapies that God provides through medical and psychological professionals as part of your overall effort to live fully and grow stronger in body, mind, and spirit during your illness journey. As one wise physician told me one day, *"Doctors treat, but only God heals."* Take advantage of all that doctors (and other professionals) can provide; they are God's children too. Just remember to always stay close to the primary source of all healing—God!

Genuinely, and in healing peace,

Richard P. Johnson

Chapter One

Depression Comes in Many "Flavors"

Just as there are many different illnesses, there are many different depressions. Perhaps it's more accurate to say that there are many different expressions of depression. I believe that there are as many different forms of depression as there are people suffering from depression. As you are certainly a unique, one-of-a-kind person, so too, the way you may experience depression is as unique as your fingerprint.

Depression robs you of your zest. It leaves you lifeless and sad, angry and irritable, stressed and easily overwhelmed. Depression twists your soul leaving you destabilized, un-centered, and unfocused, and consequently more vulnerable to slipping into your shadows and compulsions. Depression confines your personality leaving you unable to resist any noxious emotional, psychological, and spiritual forces that may accompany you when you're ill. When you're depressed you not only suffer from your diagnosed illness, all the physical pain; but also from the illness of your illness, all the emotional, psychological, and spiritual pain, as well.

Depression didn't cause your illness, but it very commonly comes along with it, and it can make your illness journey much worse. Even if you can't see the physical effects of depression, you certainly feel the emotional pain of depression, a pain that penetrates to your soul, squeezing out its essential vitality and distorting your life along with it. Depression can be torture.

Depression is a reaction to what's been called "dissonance" in your personality. Dissonance is another name for internal tension, emotional clutter, discontent, and dissension, all mixed up with the spiritual "gunpowder" of fear. In other words, depression signals an undeclared war going on in your personality. In the language of the Spiritual Strengths Healing Plan, your spiritual strengths (forces of light) are being attacked by your shadows and compulsions (forces of darkness); and there's a rising fear that the shadows and compulsions are nearing victory, or maybe even a resignation that they have already taken over.

Depression is living in a state of emotional trench warfare where you not only feel under attack, but you feel helpless to do anything about it. Depression pushes the six points of the "Law of Healing" quite out-of-reach.

When you're depressed—

1. Your beliefs lack the power for personal direction.

2. Your perceptions seem disfigured and confused.

3. Your thoughts all bend and twist around you.

4. Your feelings infect you rather than motivate you.

5. Your decisions are conflicted at best, and more likely simply frozen.

6. Your behaviors are stiff, stilted, repressed, and stifled, if not shut-down.

About Depression

Depression is primarily experienced as an affective-emotional condition, ranging on a feelings spectrum from transient unhappiness to chronic despair. Roughly one in four persons suffers from a major clinical depression at some point in life. Nearly everyone experiences "down days." Many famous people suffered from depression including religious reformer, Martin Luther; poets, Milton, Dante and Keats; philosophers Aristotle and Plato; and scientists Albert Einstein and Justice Blair, to name but a few.

The spectrum of depression ranges from mild states of common sadness, feelings of being "down," or "blue," all the way to utter despair. The duration of the minor "depressed" feelings is generally brief, lasting for a short time, sometimes hours, or a few days. On the other end of the spectrum are those who suffer from intense feelings of doom and despair, or what the psychiatric literature calls "major depression." Such sufferers experience a storm of painful feelings, and describe their condition in many ways: a pain around the heart, a bottomless abyss, a "black dog," virtual death, being spiritually dead, suffering from soul loss, dark waters rising, and the like. So-called "major depression" results when the depression hangs-on, and when the person losses a grip on the meaning of life; the depression can deepen into feelings of utter hopelessness and helplessness, and the individual loses sight of a meaningful tomorrow.

While most depression is episodic—having a beginning and an end—in some cases, depression can become chronic. When the diminished feelings become long-standing (more than one year), and when the depression is not a reaction to a current life event or loss, the depression is said to be "chronic." Generally the intensity of a chronic depression is more moderate than major depression, but more pervasive. The individual takes on a gloomy, pessimistic, negative view of the world that invades all their arenas of life.

Depression can provoke deterioration or change in daily habits. Sleep is generally disturbed: hypersomnia (excessive sleeping); insomnia, broken sleep, difficulty achieving sleep; or very early morning awakening has all been reported. The depressed individual pays less attention to personal grooming and appearance, hygiene, clothing, and the like. Frequently there is a change in housekeeping habits: increased clutter, unkempt appearance of home, general uncleanliness, and disregard for neatness are all common.

Physical and Mental Changes

Many depression sufferers complain of a chorus of physical symptoms. Common physical symptoms of depression include: heaviness of limbs, pervasive feelings of tiredness and fatigue, lowered stamina and vitality, loss of appetite (or elevated appetite), sleep disorders, and loss of sexual drive, among others almost as diverse as the disorder itself.

Cognitive changes, or mental shifts, are also common with depression; indecisiveness, mental preoccupation, and worry are frequent visitors. Mental distraction—especially created by emotional preoccupation—is commonly reported. The depressed individual may seem to be "in a fog," or "only half there." Forgetfulness, lack of follow-through, difficulty understanding instructions, inability to listen, short attention span, and general lack of attention to detail are all common in depression to one degree or another. Social isolation is almost universal among those who suffer from depression. Individuals may retreat into a self-imposed solitary confinement said to mimic the mental and emotional confinement they are experiencing. The individual seems preoccupied with inner turmoil and consequently appears decidedly self-centered.

Causes of Depression

The causes of depression are as diverse as the people who suffer from it. Feelings of depression might arise out of "thin air," or be the result of disappointments. Uninvited change, sudden loss, or accumulation of losses, anticipation of death, or fear of declining health have all been cited as "causes" of depression as well. There is no universally recognized "causal factor" of depression, variability and diversity seems the norm, yet if there is a common theme, loss of some kind seems most cited.

Illness brings with it many losses; these losses are variable depending upon the type and severity of the illness. Beyond physical losses, which of course can be devastating, illness can bring many other losses that go to the heart of one's sense of self. Illness can precipitate—

- Loss of life dreams and opportunities.

- A sense of personal defeat or failure.

- Separation from social outlets and friendships.

- Loss of personal efficiency and productivity.

- Loss of opportunity to "make a difference."

- Loss of personal status.

- Unfulfilled expectations.

Another commonly cited issue of depression is conflict in interpersonal relationships. Alienation of affection of spouse or loved ones, estrangement from family members, unresolved family conflicts, death of spouse or children, etc. are all very painful shocks to the heart of the individual.

Body, Mind, and Spirit

Depression affects the body, mind, and spirit; thus, the most effective treatment for depression involves all three.

The Body

The "chemistry of the brain" changes when a person experiences depression. The limbic system of the brain is the "seat" of your feelings, abstraction, and idea associations. Your brain, and indeed your entire nervous system, is composed of millions of **neurons** (microscopic connectors, conduits and pathways of all six functions of the personality). Neurons are separated from each other by tiny spaces called **synapses**. Each synapse is chock-full of chemicals that mediate transmission of all the messages constantly flying around the body and mind. These chemicals are called **neurotransmitters** because it is their function to facilitate communication. Several neurotransmitters, most notably norepinepherine, serotonin, and dopamine (and others) are said to be the primary "mood" chemicals because they are thought to be the primary conduits of feelings. In addition, various hormones are secreted by the hypothalamus, the pituitary gland, the adrenal glands, thyroid gland, parathyroid gland, and the pancreas, which all have chemical influence over mood states. So-called post-partum depression, suffered by some women after giving birth, results from irregularities in this hormonal mix causing imbalances in the mood stability of the individual.

The Mind

Depression negatively affects every one of the six functions of your personality...your mind. The losses mentioned above, while diminishing in themselves, are not the "culprit." What affects the mind more than the loss itself is your reaction to the **loss**. Depression can include other common emotional reactions to loss such as: anxiety, fear, fright, anger (enraged), confusion, disorientation, withdrawal, and even some level of paranoia. Many other emotional complications can emerge when a person is shocked by the diagnosis of illness. A small sampling of those feelings and memories may include:

- "Unfinished business" from former transitions or relationships
- Latent unforgiveness
- Unresolved guilt
- Bereavement
- Many personality issues
- Childhood trauma or neglect
- So-called "forgotten pain"
- Any panorama of past conflicts

These can become activated by your medical diagnosis and cause emotional and/or psychological disruption that may sow the seeds of depression.

The Spirit

Illness can rake-up some of the biggest questions of your life. Even beyond the pressing question of, *'Why is this happening to me?'* More questions of a penetrating nature emerge, *'Who am I really? Who is God for me? Where is God now? What has my life been all about? Where am I going from here? How can I make sense out of this illness?'* These and many others, so personal that most are inexpressible, or simply too unclear to even put into words, swirl through your soul seeking answers. Illness spirals you down to a starkness of living. Without a solid set of guiding-life principles, many persons with illness simply avoid the questions. When these "big questions" are put off, or they are simply too much to handle emotionally, the individual is at risk for experiencing any of the symptoms of depression already enumerated. They feel forlorn, adrift in an unfamiliar sea, floating in a confusing "soup" of meaningless never before confronted.

You can use the internal healing in your special spiritual strengths to get beyond the psychological press and emotional disruption of illness. You can harness this interior power to find relief from the ravages of depression lurking within you.

Depression as a Cry for Change

While depression can be ominously destructive when it drags on and on, it can also be a messenger of hope. Depression, however noxious, is perhaps most positively perceived as a desperate plea for relief, a cry for help, a request for assistance, and/or a desire for deep modifications. It's hard to see the core message of your depression, whatever its shape. But anger and depression are always a **request for change**. Listen to the central message of your depression; listen to whatever wisdom may be there for you. Depression allows you to learn more about who you really are at core levels of soul, shadow, and compulsion. Depression also may help you sort out the very purpose of your illness, and the hidden benefits of illness itself.

In my clinical experience I've learned that the **core message of depression** is generally hidden in plain sight, obvious once it's recognized, but for so long undecipherable in the confusing context of your everyday life. The message is always about change. The change that depression seeks may not seem at all

22

profound when it's finally unearthed and brought to light, indeed it may seem obvious and even common. It's the kind of discovery that makes you smack your head and say, '*Why didn't I see this a long time ago?*' The change always calls for a decision, and it's that decision that is so very hard.

Your Reaction to Illness

To say that you're depressed because of your illness might be a bit too superficial. Certainly your illness has rearranged your lifestyle, it has forced many, many changes that you'd much rather do without. Illness is the catalyst that first ignited your reactions to your diagnosis, but illness does NOT cause depression! What drives depression is your **reaction *to* your diagnosis** and all the life changes you've been forced to make. Depression emerges when your six personality functions of believing, perceiving, thinking, feeling, deciding, and acting (see Discover Your Spiritual Strengths for a comprehensive overview) begin to misalign. It happens when your spiritual strengths become invaded by some combination of shadows and compulsions injecting chaos into your personality.

The stress and incessant strain that you, and many persons with illness, feel from depression far outweighs any stress you may have previously encountered. The gut-wrenching ordeal of uncertainty that depression brings can pull upon you like an emotional undertow that makes you feel like you'll be sucked under at any time. When depression strikes, and especially when it hangs-on, you not only need the best medical care, you need the best psychological and spiritual care as well.

Chapter Two
Imagery, Depression, and Illness

Depression affects nearly one tenth of the American adult population at any one time; the incidence is much higher for those with illness, and for their caregivers. Depression can be triggered by trauma and/or loss, or even prolonged anxiety. People who suffer from depression generally feel trapped in a situation where they believe they are helpless.

Guided imagery for depression can help you let go of helplessness and re-vitalize your beliefs to ones of hope and other spiritual strengths. Depression may be more an emotional illness than a physical one, but it can, if left untreated, eventually lead to disease. Depression is now linked to many physical diagnoses including: osteoporosis, diabetes, heart disease, illness, and back pain (from www.healthguideinfo.com).

Imagery

Imagery is perhaps the most fundamental and simple, yet effective form of healing we have available to combat depression. You have images related to every one of your six functions of personality, and images attached to each of your spiritual strengths, shadows, and compulsions. You can learn to extinguish frightful images that your shadows and compulsions project onto you with ones that flow from your spiritual strengths. The images you construct play decisive roles in how you use your personality, how you deal with your illness, and whether you get depressed.

Images that flow from your spiritual strengths bring you peace of mind and heart, a sense of personal power (the opposite of helplessness), and an overriding felt sense of personal vitality and well-being. You can use images to strengthen your ties to your spiritual strengths, and hence to God.

I once knew a surgeon who routinely hypnotized each of his patients before surgery to control blood flow. Images let your body know what to expect. In fact, you may even be able to accelerate the functioning of your immune system simply by creating images to that effect.

You can use imaging in the Spiritual Strengths Healing Plan to help you relax, and to help "turn on" the **self-healing mechanism** of your six unique spiritual strengths. Self-healing systems in the body turn on when you truly believe that they can. Images activate your brain. Imaging may even raise the levels of the "mood chemicals" norepinepherine, serotonin, and dopamine.

Research using guided imagery with persons with cancer has consistently shown that it can reduce their length of stay in hospitals, lesson somatic symptoms such as vomiting, and reduce their need for pain meds. In fact, researcher Jeanne Achterberg of the University of Texas in Dallas found that creative imaging was the one factor that predicted cancer survival. There is ample evidence that guided imagery also reduces depression and anxiety.

Many "hard medical data" studies have supported claims of the efficacy of guided imagery with patients. Persons with illness who participate in guided imagery groups report they can share their emotions easier and increase their overall quality of life during treatment.

Both a Korean study and a very similar British study examined the effects of guided imagery used with women with breast cancer. Both studies reported increased quality of life, easier expression of emotion, and elevated mood. Studies at the Ohio College of Nursing and the University of Florida reported similar findings (from www.huffingtonpost.com/dr-tiandayton/reduce-anxiety-and-depress_b_914651.html).

Two Types of Imagery

There are two types of imagery. The first is "guided imagery" where calming and pleasant images, thoughts, and feelings are evoked to generate a state of relaxation. The second is "visualization" where the individual is brought through (either live or via recorded voice) a sequence of images, usually in story form, that provide vivid pictures of healing calm that allow the person to reframe negative images with more positive ones.

The American Cancer Society's website has this to say about imagery:

"Imagery involves mental exercises designed to allow the mind to influence the health and well-being of the body. The patient imagines sights, sounds, smells, tastes, or other sensations to create a kind of purposeful daydream. It is used with standard medical treatment in people with illness and other diseases."

The website goes on to state how their review of 46 research studies suggests that guided imagery may be helpful in a number of ways. Whereas no clear medical evidence exists to indicate that imagery directly affects cancer progression on a physical level; rich research data indicates that imagery can "help reduce stress, anxiety, and depression; manage pain, lower blood pressure; ease some of the side effects of chemotherapy; and create feelings of being in control."

The American Cancer Society states that imagery techniques are considered safe—especially under the guidance of a trained health professional, however *"relying on this type of treatment alone and avoiding or delaying conventional medical care for illness may have serious health consequences."*

Married couple O. Carl Simonton, a radiation oncologist, and Stephanie Matthews-Simonton, a psychotherapist, "perfected" one imagery technique that came to be known as the "Simonton technique." Patients were asked to imagine their bodies fighting cancer cells and winning the battle. The image used is that of the old Pac-Man characters who eat the cancer cells, just like the pac-dots from the video game.

Other "Helps" for Depression

Here are other "helps" for depression that have been researched and used to good effect:

1. Enlist the seven-step acronym AIDFARE (described below) as a way to create new images of health:

    *   Awareness that you are having a feeling.

    *   Identify (name) your feeling(s).

    *   Decide whether you want this feeling or not.

    *   Figure out what thought(s) generated this feeling.

    *   Affirm yourself with a new thought.

    *   Reassess the intensity of the feeling.

    *   Elope to peace.

2. Medication. Antidepressants can be a big help (see your doctor).
3. Seek counseling or therapy (again a huge help).
4. Avoid "sleeping in."
5. Shift your diet away from sugars and carbohydrates to more proteins.
6. Exercise. Get your body moving.
7. Get light (especially in the winter).
8. Seek the company of supportive friends.
9. Notice and change any negative "self-talk."

NOTE: If you feel you might be a threat to yourself or others, IMMEDIATELY CALL 911 AND ASK FOR ASSISTANCE.

Chapter Three
Believing, Depression, and Illness

Directions

The following page contains a "Believing Function Continuum." As truthfully and accurately as possible, circle the number on the 1-10 number line that best indicates how and what you believe about yourself at this general time in your life.

Responses 1-5 indicate relative agreement with the descriptor on the left side of the number line, while responses 6-10 indicate progressively greater agreement with the descriptor on the right side. Add up all 10 of your responses and place your total score at the bottom of the page in the space provided. This score is a very rough approximation of the level of your believing function mood right now.

Please NOTE: A clinical diagnosis of depression can only be made by a trained mental health professional.

Believing Function Continuum

My situation is hopeless.							I am hopeful things will improve.		
1	2	3	4	5	6	7	8	9	10

I have little control in my life.							I am going to fight and win.		
1	2	3	4	5	6	7	8	9	10

I have come to expect the worst.							I believe good will happen.		
1	2	3	4	5	6	7	8	9	10

Things won't change.							Tomorrow things will be different.		
1	2	3	4	5	6	7	8	9	10

My personality is lacking.							My personality is blessed.		
1	2	3	4	5	6	7	8	9	10

I lack enthusiasm in my life.							I live with a lot of enthusiasm.		
1	2	3	4	5	6	7	8	9	10

I dread each day.							I look forward to each day.		
1	2	3	4	5	6	7	8	9	10

I have little faith in myself.							I have a lot of faith in my abilities.		
1	2	3	4	5	6	7	8	9	10

I am unmotivated.							I am very motivated.		
1	2	3	4	5	6	7	8	9	10

Depression is fundamental to me.							Joy is fundamental to me.		
1	2	3	4	5	6	7	8	9	10

My total "believing" affect score is _____.

You can now go to page 115 and transfer this total score onto the respective number line you see there.

Believing, Depression, and Illness

Whether you are depressed or not...whether you have illness or not...you are still a piece of God's perfection, just like a flower, or a leaf, or sunshine, or clean water.

What are you? What's your conception of you? What and who do you believe you are? Are you a body living in a physical world and striving for a spiritual reality, or are you essentially a spiritual entity living in a physical world dealing with the laws of the material that hold sway here? The answers you give to these questions are at the heart of how you approach the illness in your life and any depression that may come along with it.

The first function of your personality is to believe (see <u>Discover Your Spiritual Strengths</u>, pages 65 to 76). You have millions of beliefs, some of which come together into bundles (several or many) to form your attitudes. Depression forces you to believe in more negative ways, and hence form negative attitudes. Getting beyond depression requires you to modify these negative attitudes. You need to change attitudes to usher in permanent change.

A good example of this might be dieting. For a diet to bring about lasting weight reduction and ongoing weight loss maintenance, you need to change your very attitudes about food and about eating. You need to come up with new and healthier answers to two basic questions: (1) What is food? (2) What is the behavior of eating? The degree to which you succeed in creating new and healthier answers to these questions and go on to incorporate your new answers as fundamental parts of your belief core, is the degree to which you will achieve your weight loss goals.

Reliance on God does eventually heal you.

The same is true for illness and depression. What are the attitudes that you need to change about illness and depression? Your function here on this earth is bigger than the world you see; you are drawn to the central power of God that also exists inside of you. Using this notion as a basic belief shifts your attitudes in ways that form the basic foundation of how to best deal with depression.

You can train yourself to listen to the teacher in your soul who is constantly instructing you how to live best in whatever situation you happen to find yourself. This voice speaks of peace and offers another meaning of illness. During your illness journey, regularly consult your **inner teacher**.

Everything that confronts you in your world contains potential life-learning. God wants you to be happy—perhaps not happiness as the world defines it—but the genuine and joyful happiness of knowing, deeply knowing that you are loved. The challenge of making this central belief or value part of your belief core is a huge step in dealing with any depression that comes your way.

You can learn to replace any noxious emotions such as fear, anger, revenge, guilt, and contempt with hope, gratitude, and the other spiritual strengths in this program. These all flow from love, and love is your inheritance from God. Bitterness and other forms of sadness and fear are merely places of absence of love in your heart, and an absence is not really real. The **true reality** is always love, therefore love, in all its forms, becomes your only goal.

God, the power and source of all healing, lives in you...in your spiritual strengths.

You can come to believe the simple truth that everything has a purpose, even your illness, by looking past the worldly image it presents and instead investing yourself in a more accurate belief that exists beyond the pain. This lesson is always available; the love is always there for you to hold firm.

When the foundation for your beliefs is not set in love, then you place your lot with fear and ultimately experience only pain. Your body is a vehicle, a means of communication, a way to connect with other souls who are likewise in a body like you are. Your body must have a purpose, and because illness exists it too must also have a purpose. What is the purpose of your illness?

Moving beyond illness requires that you expand your belief system. You have the power to do this, to change your very beliefs and the attitudes they spawn. Your illness journey is asking you to change your beliefs, but it takes concentration and work. What you believe is what you eventually will perceive. Therefore, **whatever you believe creates your own reality**.

You are part of God's creation, and creation is abundant; it lacks nothing. You can tap into the abundance because God, who is whole and complete, lives within you. Your beliefs about what and who you are, and what and who you can be, determine what you will be.

What is most important for you? Your health, your finances, your longevity, your family, friends, career...what? The foundational ethical, moral, and practical judgments you make about what's important will determine what is of value to you. When you're struggling with illness, you need all the awareness you can muster...you need to be alert, awake, and ready in full measure to learn the gifts our your illness journey and learn them well. What have you decided to believe in: failure or success?

The equation of love in your heart and soul is unlike any other.

In his book <u>Unlimited Power</u>, Anthony Robbins, thinker, presenter, entrepreneur, author, and human potential enthusiast, gives us six beliefs that he recognizes as necessary and sufficient for success in life. His definition of success is "the ongoing process of striving to become more." I think I would modify this definition to "the ongoing process to become who you authentically are." Nonetheless, here are Robbins' six key empowering beliefs:

1. Everything happens for a reason and a purpose and everything that happens serves us.

2. There is no such thing as failure, there are only results.

3. Whatever happens...take responsibility!

4. It's not necessary to understand everything to be able to use everything.

5. People are your greatest resource.

6. Work is play.

You have a life that is beyond your senses.

What are your **key empowering beliefs**? Your body is in this world and also of this world; your body then is governed by the material (physical) laws of this world. The real you, your genuine, authentic reality is also <u>in</u> this world, but it is not <u>of</u> this world. The real you (soul) is not governed by the rules and laws of the natural world like your body, but rather by the mysterious spiritual reality of the divine. Your illness is of this world and can only affect that which is of this world...your illness cannot diminish the real you…but you can learn and grow from the lessons of your illness.

There is great tension between the body and the mind, and the soul. Yet, this tension is good; out of this tension emerges (sometimes painfully) the "new you," the transformed you, the "you" that is closer to who you truly are. The more you identify with (believe in) the physical definition of you, i.e., your body, the more vulnerable you are to the ravages of depression.

Each Monday is Your "Believing" Day

What follows are two guided imagery sequences and one healing prayer specially designed to keep anger and depression at bay. Each of these is focused toward the believing function of your personality. In the Spiritual Strengths Seven-Week Healing Immersion Program, Monday is always your believing function day, and so it's recommended that you go through the two guided imagery sequences (below), and follow each with the healing prayer each Monday. You might want to go through one guided imagery sequence in the morning and the second in the afternoon or evening. The same consideration will be given to the other functions on other days (Tuesday is perceiving; Wednesday is thinking; Thursday is feeling; Friday is deciding; and Saturday is acting).

You might want to begin the guided imagery sequences by first going through a mental relaxation procedure that will cleanse you of undue stress and tension and thereby allow you to be more fully receptive to the guided imagery. You can use the same relaxation procedure with all guided imagery sequences in this book.

Simple Relaxation Sequence Procedure

1. Wherever you are, arrange your body, clothing, and posture so you are maximally comfortable.

2. Imagine a point of light on the very top of your head. This point of light is God's healing power.

3. Imagine this point of light growing larger and larger until it covers your entire scalp—then your entire face. Mentally relax all the muscles "under" this expanding light.

4. Imagine the muscles on the back of your neck. In your mind's eye "see" these neck muscles on either side of your neck vertebrae as made up of thousands of tiny muscle fibers that look like small rubber bands that are stretched tight and taut. You notice that as these muscle fibers begin to relax, they release extremely tiny droplets of what looks like black ink. This is the "black bile" of stress that, once released, begins draining down your neck, your back, and right out of you.

5. Imagine the light of God's grace slowly covering your entire body and releasing the "black bile" of stress in all your muscles throughout your body.

You are now poised to fully experience the following healing imagery sequences.

Beliefs

Guided Healing Imagery 1

Imagine yourself as a 6 year old in the house where you lived then.

You look around...feel the feelings you felt then.

But your parents are not there. You realize you are alone and you feel as empty as the house.

The house is empty...cold, stark, scary.

You become confused and afraid.

You run out and go down to your town center.

You go in all the stores, you old school, the library...but no one is there!

You're frantic...chaos overtakes your soul.

After stumbling around in abject insecurity—trembling down to your very soul—you collapse on the lawn in front of the church.

The grass is smooth and green, it smells wonderful, you can hear the birds, and you feel the sunshine on your face.

You open your eyes and see a white marble in the grass.

You pick it up. You notice it is glowing.

Instinctively and without hesitation, you place the white marble on the very top of your head, the place where all your beliefs reside.

There it shines and glows and fills the emptiness that was there.

The glowing light from the marble completely surrounds you.

It overpowers the doubt; it outshines the darkness; it penetrates the fear.

The light brings hope, trust, and certainty along with it.

With renewed spirit and clearer resolve, you feel exhilarated and vitalized.

You run back to your house.

You find that your parents are there.

They embrace you...you feel safe in their arms.

You realize that all the fear, the deep sadness, and the sorrowful guilt that you formerly felt has now completely melted away.

Beliefs

Guided Healing Imagery 2

Imagine a small white round marble hovering about one inch above the top of your head. This marble is the receptor site for all of God's healing power/grace from your believing spiritual strength (God-Reliance, Humility, Acceptance, Mercy, or Hope). You notice that the white marble is very tarnished, dirty, blemished, dull, and generally covered in a rust-like corrosion that completely blocks out God's healing power and grace from getting through.

To remedy the situation, you decide to descend to the fountain of healing water in your soul. Your soul is deep within you—accessed only by a long spiral stairway.

You enter the stairway through an entry opening directly under the hovering white marble above your head. The bright beam from your flashlight pierces the inky blackness of the stairway. The stairway is made of stone...stone steps circling round and round, with stone wall sides. There is nothing on the walls to indicate how far you've descended.

You begin your descent and you very quickly notice that with every new turn, indeed with every step you take, you feel sensations of stress and tension draining away from you; you feel your mood ascending the farther you descend down the stairs. While you're a bit timid in your descent down the stairway, you're confident that you will reach your soul.

After a long time climbing down, down, and down farther, you finally reach the bottom step. As you swing your flashlight around, you realize that you are in an ante chamber all made of the same stone as the stairway. The room isn't large, but it also isn't small. The room is plain in that nothing adorns the walls. Then you notice a large oak double door on the other side of the room. As you approach it, you marvel at its intricate carving and polished surface—it's a magnificent door.

You reach out for the bronze handle and with little effort, the beautiful door begins opening. It reveals what appears to be a chapel—indeed, the most beautiful chapel you've ever seen. As you begin walking down the center isle toward the altar, your eyes are drawn to a gorgeous fountain. Six streams flow from the center of the fountain pool, each stream arches to the outer edge of the round fountain pool. These are the six streams of grace pouring into your personality: believing, perceiving, thinking, feeling, deciding, and acting streams. Without hesitation, you lift a clear crystal decanter from a small table next to the fountain and fill it with water coming from the "believing" stream. Immediately you take the filled water decanter with you out of the chapel into the ante-room and begin climbing the long spiral stairway up, up, and up.

After what seems a very long time climbing, and just before you are ready to collapse from exhaustion, you see the light of day at the top of the stairs. You rest a bit on a bench right outside of the entrance of the stairway, holding the filled crystal decanter beside you on the bench. The sun is shining warm and bright, and you feel tired but emotionally exhilarated.

You're very thirsty so you decide to take a drink from the decanter. As soon as you do, you notice that the white marble still hovering above your head begins to miraculously shed its encrusted corrosion from its surface; all dirt, and grime, and "junk" seems to melt away leaving the white marble clean, polished, lustrous, and so very beautiful.

Once clean the white marble immediately becomes reactivated and begins receiving God's believing healing grace/power with renewed and full capacity. You experience a surge of healing power within you which immediately lifts your spirits, and greatly relieves any sense of depression you formerly felt. Beyond this, in your mind's eye, you can see your newly invigorated believing spiritual strength surrounding any traces of your illness (or other brokenness) and eating it up.

Believing Prayer

Let me, Lord

Let me merely close my eyes and forget all I thought I knew and understood.

Let me endeavor to relinquish every belief that clutters up my mind and serves to keep me chained to this world.

Let me give over every attitude, value, expectation, or assumption that blocks me from reason, sanity, and truth.

Let me challenge all idle beliefs and exchange them for beliefs of peace, love, forgiveness, and compassion.

Let me place myself in your charge Lord; let me give away silly illusions, wishful assumptions, and valueless attitudes.

Let me better understand the virtue of peace, and the values of genuine healing and forgiveness more clearly.

Let me become aware in keen recognition of all the things I saved to settle for myself, and therefore kept away from your healing and my spiritual strengths within, Lord.

Let me lean my head against your shoulder and rest awhile and find the peace that you've already placed within me.

Let the ancient door to my soul swing free again, and let me listen to the echoes of love in my deepest memory.

Amen

Chapter Four

Perceiving, Depression, and Illness

Directions

The following page contains a "Perceiving Function Continuum." As truthfully and accurately as possible, circle the number on the 1-10 number line that best indicates how and what you believe about yourself at this general time in your life.

Responses 1-5 indicate relative agreement with the descriptor on the left side of the number line, while responses 6-10 indicate progressively greater agreement with the descriptor on the right side. Add up all 10 of your responses and place your total score at the bottom of the page in the space provided. This score is a very rough approximation of the level of your perceiving function mood right now.

Please NOTE: A clinical diagnosis of depression can only be made by a trained mental health professional.

Perceiving Function Continuum

I perceive loss.								I perceive gains.	
1	2	3	4	5	6	7	8	9	10

My outlook is disheartened.						I see life as vital and vibrant.			
1	2	3	4	5	6	7	8	9	10

I have a gloomy view.					I have a bright and cheerful view.				
1	2	3	4	5	6	7	8	9	10

Darkness blocks my vision.							Light clears my vision.		
1	2	3	4	5	6	7	8	9	10

I question my perceptions.						I trust my perceptions.			
1	2	3	4	5	6	7	8	9	10

I see myself as a loner.								I like groups.	
1	2	3	4	5	6	7	8	9	10

My best times are spoiled.							My best times are vital.		
1	2	3	4	5	6	7	8	9	10

I have a disappointed point of view.						I have an upbeat and accurate point of view.			
1	2	3	4	5	6	7	8	9	10

I have a dispirited point of view.					I have an uplifting point of view.				
1	2	3	4	5	6	7	8	9	10

It's hard for me to see the Light.					It's easy for me to see the Light.				
1	2	3	4	5	6	7	8	9	10

My total "perceiving" affect score is _____.

You can now go to page 115 and transfer this total score onto the respective number line you see there.

46

How Do You Perceive Illness?

During your illness journey, you're being called to develop new spiritual **insight** as well as a new spiritual **outlook**. Your perceiving function spiritual strength is God's power within you, the power necessary to see the farther horizon of God's infinite love even in your illness.

Your job is to **reframe your illness** in such a way that there is no room for depression. You can rearrange your perspective and discover new ways of "viewing" your illness. When you confuse levels of perception: physical, mental, and spiritual, it's then you start to slip into your shadows and compulsions and feel depressed.

Illness is both a fact of your life and an event in your life. What you do with the events in your life is to "perceive" them. Events are, by themselves, quite neutral until you do something with them, and the first thing you do is perceive them. Your awareness of what is real, important, and what has value and priority in your life, always aligns with your beliefs.

Your life is guided, perhaps even directed, by your beliefs and attitudes, or as we say it in psychology: your beliefs are the mother of your actions. The first step in giving meaning to any event, circumstance, relationship, etc. in your life is to perceive it. How do you perceive illness, and how do you perceive depression?

View your depression as a path that eventually leads you to God and to healing.

Is there a way of looking at illness and depression, indeed everything in your life, as **another step toward God**, another movement toward love? How can you put on new eyes and "see" differently? Gerald Jampolsky, M.D., psychiatrist and author, instructs us that whenever we feel down, or sad, beleaguered, or depressed, say to yourself, "*I could see this differently.*" (Love is Letting Go of Fear). This simple little notion is profound; the possibility that you don't have to be confined to any one way of seeing anything, thus freeing yourself from the tyranny of thinking that you're stuck in this depressed feeling state forever. You are not!

You can fall into the awareness trap of seeing your illness and depression only as a contradiction of God's promise of abundance. Abundance means "everything," which includes even the things you don't think of as particularly good. God wants you to experience everything...all of it.

The wisdom here is that unless you experience (perceive) the **abundance** of everything; you cannot gain the necessary outlook (perception) to know the value of what is of love and what is of fear. Seeing your illness as a disharmony, or some trick that's being perpetrated upon you, or a bad dream, or a betrayal of some sort, or even a punishment of some proportion, can lead you away from the truth of love within you—the very love that God wants for you that is most clearly seen (perceived) in your six premier spiritual strengths.

Your depression may be the secret channel through which the Holy Spirit pours infinite healing...your suffering then has purpose.

How can you change your perception of illness, anger, and depression in such a way that they become a way of letting the light of heaven shine in? Using the Spiritual Strengths Healing Plan, you learn how to move away from shadows and compulsions and toward your perceiving spiritual strength. If you desire peace of mind and heart, if you desire harmony of soul, if you desire to participate in becoming "brand new," then shifting your perceptions is mandatory. You need to walk over the bridge of forgiveness, leaving former perceptions of misery and contention behind, to find happiness on the other side.

Viewing your body as the only reality is a deception. Your body is certainly real, but there is so much **more to the real "you"** than body. Your body is tangible, your body is physical, but the whole you is body (physical), mind (mental), and soul (spiritual).

All things physical are subject to the diminishing forces of nature, most notably oxidation and combustion. Your body is oxidizing, rusting out, and combusting, burning up, every day that you live. Illness is but an acceleration of these two forces of physical destruction, a process of bringing the materials of your body back to the earth. This process evokes sadness, but it's as natural as is the growth of a tomato plant.

Can you see the whole you? Although it too is an intangible entity, you can probably see (perceive) your mind as real because there is so much energy given to education across the lifespan. But **can you see** the spiritual you, the numinous parts of you, as being equally, or even more real than your body and your mind? Illness, especially when accompanied by anger and depression, propels you to change your perception of healing. When you pray to God for healing, what do you mean and what does God hear? Your perception of healing involves things of this world; God's perception of healing involves things of the divine...of the spirit.

Partial Vision

Most of the time, you, like most of us, engage in partial vision. You look through a small knothole in a wooden fence and **make assumptions** about the whole of reality only by what you see through that tiny little hole. Healing requires that we see the broader view, a fuller perspective. You are called to see your illness from the viewpoint of your spiritual strengths, and especially your perceiving strength. Otherwise you're stuck in the blindedness of your perceiving shadow and compulsion—both of which confine your perception to tiny snippets of reality that leave your vision in poverty and your understanding lacking. This **perceptual insufficiency** sets you up for depression. Only when you develop the willingness to receive the gift of true sight will you be unburdened of the pain of fear.

How you frame (perceive) events, and in what context, changes how you receive them. For example, hearing footsteps in the night in your kitchen when you're in bed upstairs has a completely different meaning than hearing footsteps while walking along a sidewalk in broad daylight on a busy street. Another example is the difference between the two women who stayed a weekend at a very elegant hotel. One described her visit as "miserable" because on Saturday night the waiter scowled at the maître-de all evening. The second woman described her stay as "marvelous." *"There was even a little intrigue going on between our waiter and the maître-de on Saturday night,"* she exclaimed. Both women experienced the same hotel, the same service, food and amenities, yet each came away with opposite opinions because each framed (saw) the experience differently. They were coming from two completely separate frames of reference and consequently solidified two very different realities about the weekend.

Depression is a time to walk in the darkness, knowing that along the way God's healing grace/power is saturating your personality for a new tomorrow.

Only when you try to see your illness as God sees it will the **veil be lifted** on its true purpose, all else stops you short of whole meaning. The first step is coming to trust the Spirit within you, which opens you to true healing power. Your illness may be shifting your perception of your body from one illusion to another.

Before your illness, you viewed your body as the source of all earthly pleasure; this myopic vision of your body ensured that pursuing your "creature comforts" remained the central focus of your life. Now, after your diagnosis, you may have shifted to another equally illusionary perspective of your body as the source of all evil for you, the core of all anguish, the seat of fear, and the source of all attack. Healing means transforming your view of your body: seeing it as a teaching aid, and as a porthole of deeper illumination and understanding.

Spiritual Vision

Give as much consistent effort as you can to seeing the future as belonging to God—only God has power over it...not you. There is nothing more you can do to see accurately than seeking the peace of God. Without God, illness may only bring you pain, disappointment, despair, doubt, and hopelessness. Until you move toward seeing all as blessed, you will be frustrated and bound to the incomplete vision of this world.

The first step to developing this **spiritual *vision*** actually entails using a different sense altogether. It involves *listening* as closely as possible. Who or what do you listen to? Developing vision requires that you regularly consult with God in prayer. If you feel unqualified or rusty at prayer, I recommend you read <u>Healing Prayers</u> (one of the books in the Spiritual Strengths Inner Healing Series library).

Prayer involves listening to God's voice within you as well as talking to God. Some people have a very difficult time reaching a state of peace and relaxation necessary to achieve prayerful listening. To improve your listening in prayer, you might want to first work on using progressive muscle relaxation as a means to center you like the simple relaxation sequence procedure covered on page 38 of the previous chapter.

Depression quiets your exterior life so that dramatic healing can work its full "magic" in your very busy interior.

In addition, to help you focus on the Spirit's voice as you move deeper into relaxation, you may want to use some affirmations like those in another Spiritual Strengths Healing book, Healing Wisdom. Use these kinds of centering statements on a daily basis to sharpen your vision as well as better align with your spiritual strengths. Your goal is to move yourself toward spiritual awakening, a fuller awareness of God's presence within. Reframing your perceptions so that you can see in God's holy light will bring you ever closer to your healing goal.

Perception

Guided Healing Imagery 1

In your mind's eye you see a small child in a cozy log cabin in the deep forest.

The child's father is there, too.

The scene is so tender...

The fire is glowing...

They are making hot chocolate and popcorn.

The child (who is you at age five) is dressed in fleece-lined slippers, pajamas, and a flannel bathrobe.

Your father has a pipe, and a red flannel shirt.

The two sit together...you on your father's lap in front of the fire.

You feel the penetrating warmth of the fire...

You smell the popcorn,

You hear the crackle of the fire,

Your father's shirt is so soft,

You taste the hot chocolate.

Suddenly, you both hear a strange noise outside in the rain and wind.

Your father reassures you as he puts on his overcoat, boots, and hat...

He'll be right back after he checks the noise.

At first you remain confident as you climb back into the easy chair...

But, as the time lengthens and the fire dies to embers...

You begin to feel the chill,

Not only are you physically cold because of the dying fire...

You also feel the shiver of fear, which starts to ascend up your back.

The kerosene lamp now dies due to lack of fuel...

The quickly dying fire is the only spark of light in the cabin.

Fear now grips the air like ominous icicles hanging from a mortuary doorway.

Somehow you gather the courage to slowly walk to the front window.

Silently you pull back the curtain to reveal the rain bleating on the window pane so no one could see in or out of the watery distortion formed there...

The chill of fear now escalates to a pre-panic...

The wind is swirling and bumping the porch furniture to and fro; a frantic feeling of desperation stuns you and begins to overtake your emotions.

You're now cold and empty...forlorn and forgotten...alone and fearful.

Beyond your fear, a new idea emerges...

You are not alone. God is there with you always—always!

But your perception is distorted as you strain to see through the window.

Suddenly, there on the windowsill, you spy a small white marble. It glows and somehow beckons you to it.

You pick it up, and for some unknown reason you press it against your eyes.

It immediately penetrates into your eyeballs.

The luminosity of the marble clears your vision.

You look out the window and can see your father lying at the base of the steps to the cabin.

You rush out into the storm and shake him awake.

Slowly he struggles to his feet.

With your arm around his waist to steady him, you help him in the cabin.

He's soaked and exhausted, but he's OK.

He tells you that he had slipped on the steps and must have hit his head on the stairs in the fall, knocking him out.

He tells you that you saved his life.

He cleans himself up, restarts the fire, and warms the hot chocolate.

He settles back into his easy chair where you cuddle on his lap.

And all is well again.

Perception

Guided Healing Imagery 2

Imagine a small white round marble embedded in your eyes. These two marbles are the receptor sites for all of God's healing power/grace from your perceiving spiritual strength (Vision, Humor, Peace, Adaptability, or Simplicity). You notice that the white marbles are very tarnished, dirty, blemished, dull, and generally covered in a rust-like corrosion that completely blocks out God's healing power/grace from getting through.

To remedy the situation, you decide to descend to the fountain of healing water in your soul. Your soul is deep within you accessed only by a long spiral stairway.

You enter the stairway through an entry opening directly under the believing white marble that hovers above your head. The bright beam from your flashlight pierces the inky blackness of the stairway. The stairway is all made of stone...stone steps circling round and round, with stone wall covering the sides. There is nothing on the walls to indicate how far you've descended.

You begin your descent and very quickly notice that with every new turn, indeed with every step you take, you feel sensations of stress and tension lifting from you; you feel your mood ascending the farther you descend down the stairs. While you're a bit timid in your descent down the stairway, you're confident that you will reach your soul.

After a long time of climbing down, down, and down farther, you finally reach the bottom step. As you swing your flashlight around, you realize that you are in an ante chamber all made of the same stone as the stairway. The room isn't large, but it also isn't small. The room is plain in that nothing adorns the walls. Then you notice a large oak double door on the other side of the room. As you approach it, you marvel at its intricate carving and polished surface—it's a magnificent door.

You reach out for the bronze handle and with little effort, the beautiful door begins opening. It reveals what appears to be a chapel—the most beautiful chapel you've ever seen. You begin walking down the center isle toward the altar, when your eyes are drawn to a gorgeous fountain. Six streams flow from the very center of the fountain pool, one for each of the six functions of your personality. Each stream arches out to the outer edge of the round fountain pool. These are the believing, perceiving, thinking, feeling, deciding, and acting streams. Without hesitation, you lift a clear crystal decanter from the small table next to the fountain and fill it with water coming from the "<u>perceiving</u>" stream. Immediately you take the filled water decanter with you out of the chapel into the ante-room and begin climbing the long spiral stairway up, up, and up.

After a long and arduous climb, and just before you are ready to collapse from exhaustion, you see the light of day at the top of the stairs. You rest a bit on a bench right outside of the entrance of the stairway, holding the filled crystal decanter beside you on the bench. The sun is shining warm and bright, and you feel tired but emotionally exhilarated.

You're thirsty so you decide to take a drink from the decanter. As soon as you do, the white marbles embedded in your eyes begin to miraculously begin shedding the encrusted corrosion from their surfaces; all dirt, and smear, and grime, and "junk" seems to melt away leaving the white marbles clean, polished, lustrous, and so very beautiful.

Once clean, the white marbles immediately become reactivated and begin receiving God's perceiving healing grace/power with renewed and full capacity. You experience a surge of healing power within you that appears to greatly relieve any sense of depression you formerly felt. Beyond this, in your mind's eye, you can see your newly invigorated perceiving spiritual strength surrounding any traces of your illness (or other brokenness) and eating it up.

Perceiving Prayer

Help Me See, Lord

Join your mind with the minds of all your brothers and sisters who are praying for healing just like you.

Repeat God's name and all the tiny, senseless things of this world slip into true and right perspective. Repeat God's name and see how quickly you forget those things you formerly valued but which now you realize have only little, if any meaning.

God cannot hear requests that are not of Love. God can only hear requests that are in harmony with divine laws.

Listen and begin to open to the healing power within; invite the Holy Spirit in to illuminate your sight and transform your perception into true vision—to see through God's eyes.

Call upon God's name, which is your name, and recognize that you can touch the healing power within.

Lord, help me bring healing to my perception so I may see all things accurately. My condemnation and lack of forgiveness keeps my vision dark; and through my sightless eyes, I cannot see the vision of the glory you have waiting for me, Lord.

Today I can behold this glory and be glad. Remind me, Lord, now for I am weary of the world I see. Reveal what you would have me see instead.

Amen

Chapter Five
Thinking, Depression, and Illness

Directions

The following page contains a "Thinking Function Continuum." As truthfully and accurately as possible, circle the number on the 1-10 number line that best indicates how and what you believe about yourself at this general time in your life.

Responses 1-5 indicate relative agreement with the descriptor on the left side of the number line, while responses 6-10 indicate progressively greater agreement with the descriptor on the right side. Add up all 10 of your responses and place your total score at the bottom of the page in the space provided. This score is a very rough approximation of the level of your thinking function mood right now.

Please NOTE: A clinical diagnosis of depression can only be made by a trained mental health professional.

Thinking Function Continuum

My thinking is pessimistic.   My thinking is optimistic.

     1   2   3   4   5   6   7   8   9   10

My future seems bleak.   My future looks fulfilling.

     1   2   3   4   5   6   7   8   9   10

My thinking is distressed.   My thinking is upbeat.

     1   2   3   4   5   6   7   8   9   10

I have no praiseworthy traits.   I have very valuable traits.

     1   2   3   4   5   6   7   8   9   10

I judge myself harshly.   I judge myself lightly.

     1   2   3   4   5   6   7   8   9   10

Others don't understand my pain.   Others understand to my pain.

     1   2   3   4   5   6   7   8   9   10

I think only of my own plights.   I think of others before myself.

     1   2   3   4   5   6   7   8   9   10

I don't think very clearly.   I enjoy clarity of thought.

     1   2   3   4   5   6   7   8   9   10

I have lots of aches and pains.   I am relatively pain free.

     1   2   3   4   5   6   7   8   9   10

I magnify personal failures.   I keep a good perspective.

     1   2   3   4   5   6   7   8   9   10

My total "thinking" affect score is _____.

You can now go to page 115 and transfer this total score onto the respective number line you see there.

Thoughts and Healing

Henry Ford once said, *"Don't find fault...find a remedy."* This simple but profound statement could be the slogan for all persons with any illness who sincerely want to change, want to live the best they can, want to feel good, and perhaps most importantly, know that their thoughts have great impact on their healing.

Thoughts are your **internal communications**, they are what you say to your*self*; what you do in your life is determined by what you say to your*self*. You lack no healing resources and **you lack no healing power**; what you may lack, however, is control over those resources. Perhaps you even deny yourself access to the power of the Divine that resides within you. Your thoughts are the key to access the treasure deep inside you that contains the riches of the universe for you. What do you say to yourself about illness...about healing...about healing power...about your relationships with God?

Depression may be your call from God to remain simple and pliable, but also steadfast in courage knowing that the Holy Spirit continuously nudges you toward healing.

You can direct your thoughts in any direction you wish. Once you are aware that your thinking is under your own influence and that your thoughts are not likes corks on a tempestuous sea being tossed this way and that, you can become more aware of what and how you are thinking and grab the harness of your thinking, steering it toward your spiritual strengths and away from your shadows and compulsions. You are in charge of whether your thoughts are consumed by the lower or bodily level of your experience (shadows and compulsions), or the higher or spiritual level of your experience (spiritual strengths). The choice is yours.

Your job is to gradually place your thoughts in service of the Holy Spirit. Your mind can elect what it chooses to serve.

To change your mind, as you must do in order to heal, means to place your spiritual strengths as the "thought leaders" of your mind.

When your focus on the world and the things of the world is chronically critical, this makes you blind to what lies beyond it...your healing. Without this insight, your **thoughts are trapped** in confusion, misery and death. Let the thought of God saturate you. The thought of God made you and can never leave you—it is the source of your life...the beginning and the end that has no end. The fullness of the cosmos shines within you and brings joy and health, peace and harmony, delight and security to a mind weary of focusing only on a tired world.

You can train your mind to lay aside denial, and **accept the thought** that comes from your center, your core. The very power of God is in you in a place where there is no poverty, no diminishment, no illness, no anger, and no depression. Tap into this place and receive healing. You are the only one who can cut yourself off from the majestic flow of energy. No, you are not worthy to receive God, but God can only say the word and you will be healed, if you can open the windows of your soul and let the light of healing in.

Depression, and your walk with illness, may be your most sacred time.

You need to **change your mind** about so much, but perhaps the first thing that needs modification is your thinking about your purpose on this earth, and the personal meaning that flows from this purpose. What are you here to accomplish? For example, ask yourself what is troubling you now. Whatever it may be, you will think of it differently when you close your eyes and come up with a new meaning for the trouble...this will bring you peace. Peace is one of the central goals of life, contention and contradiction are its opposites that bring only a fraudulent sense of purpose, but there is no true mission in this purpose, only turmoil and tumult. You can change your mind by practicing this simple little statement:

"This thought I don't want. Instead I choose to think   ."

This of course is not a panacea, but when practiced regularly it will shift your thinking away from the false and insecure thoughts of your shadows and compulsions and toward the sure stability of your spiritual strengths. You need to learn to place the future in the hands of God...to shift your thinking and become as accurate as possible. Healing requires that you become more aware of the thoughts that rule your mind; especially the ones that bring you into darkness and cause you only rage and defeat. An **un-centered mind** leads you to confusion and error...you become lost most of the time, you become fixated on what is not truth, and you lay aside what is truth. It's no wonder that your healing is anemic and your understanding of life is likewise.

Your body is flesh; is there any question then that it will eventually let you down? Could there be any other outcome for your body on this plane other than this disappointment? When you were younger your body was everything, you thought it invincible; you thought it the center of your world. Now your body may seem a heavy and almost unnecessary appendage; certainly it is not only this, it is so much more. Yet, your body seems to plague you with ever-shriller demands for more and more care. How could you place your trust in your body when it's so fragile?

Attach your thoughts to love, the central and invincible power of the cosmos. You are healed when your thoughts no longer connect your overall well-being with your body. When accurate thinking prevails in your mind and in your heart, you will be healed, there will be no more reason to hang on to a definition of yourself that starts and ends with your body. On that day you will graduate from scarcity to abundance of spirit.

One way God heals is through paradox...your distress may paradoxically carry out an unknown divine design.

Your mind is not a captive of the bag of bones (your body) that you carry around wherever you go. Your mind is free to roam the highways and byways of your consciousness—selecting only the best thoughts like a connoisseur of fine wine selects only the best for his closest friends.

Dr. David Burns, M.D., psychiatrist and bestselling author (Feeling Good, The New Mood Therapy), suggested so many years ago that you need to **get out of the judgment business**. A thought cannot be neutral: it is an evaluation, a judgment that speaks of condemnation, or it is a statement of learning; it is recognizing love in action that speaks of forgiveness. There is no middle course. Accurate thinking doesn't judge, it doesn't condemn, it only thinks of the wonder of God's creation in each and every one of God's creations.

Your mind is split between the undeserved spiritual strengths that are always taking root in your mind on the one hand, and the treacherous thinking spawned by your shadows and compulsions on the other. This split keeps you in confusion, and pushes you away from the altar of understanding within you—away from learning God's healing laws.

Learned Helplessness

Experiments done with animals by researcher Dr. Martin Seligman eventuated in a new theory of human behavior known as "learned helplessness." Dr. Seligman suggests that we learn helplessness when we are repeatedly exposed to various levels of "shock." Seligman's early experiments involved shocking animals (dogs) in a specially constructed "experimental" box affixed with an electric current running through the metal floor grid of the box so that the animal could not avoid the shock. Initially the animals frantically attempted to avoid the shock, but after some duration the animal realized that escape was impossible and became resigned to the shock without further resistance. After several administrations of this treatment, the shocked animals became docile to the point of inactivity even when the box was modified so that escape was possible. The dogs simply became depressed and apparently helpless. Dr. Seligman dubbed this "learned helplessness" and soon after applied this discovery to humans.

How strange that depression may pave the way
for you to ultimately embrace healing.

Illness can be seen as a repeated physical and emotional "shock" that cannot be avoided. After a time, the patient simply resigns to frustration by becoming docile, dismayed, and depressed. Further research with illness patients indicates that adopting this helpless emotional posture can actually interfere with the normal and natural resistance to the illness, on both physical and emotional levels, probably best known as a "fighting spirit." Depression then can be seen as a form of "learned helplessness" that depletes your stamina to carry on. Breaking this unfortunate spiral of conditioning is difficult but is the goal of this thinking function of the personality.

Simple Relaxation Sequence Procedure

Before you move onto the following guided-imagery sequences, you'll want to prepare your mind, heart, and soul by going through the simple relaxation sequence procedure described on page 38.

Thoughts

Guided Healing Imagery 1

You are six years old.

You are in the living room of your house and realize that you are alone.

A sense of uneasiness and disquietude comes over you.

You hear strange noises upstairs...you see shadows on the wall.

You feel a chill rising up your spine.

You decide to look for your parents and walk out onto the dark sidewalk.

From around the corner, you see a shape that looks like your father.

You call to him and run to reach him as he rounds yet another corner in the darkness.

Frightened, you pursue him faster.

At last you see him as he's about to lurch into the corner tavern.

You follow him in, hesitating to find your courage since you've never been in the tavern before and it looks like a foreboding place.

As the door closes behind you, your senses are filled.

Brassy music...cigar smoke...wet floor.

Disapproving faces turn toward you.

You feel the sharp corner of the table as you back into it.

You smell the putrid odor of stale beer.

Body humidity fills the air.

You feel the cold anticipation of panic as your eyes dart to find no sign of your father.

You're alone again.

But worse than alone...

Fear streaks silently within you as a gaunt man grabs your shoulder...

"What are you doing here?" he demands.

Your thoughts begin to race with frantic recklessness.

Uncontrolled, your thoughts echo the emptiness you feel inside.

Thoughts seem to overtake whatever peace might have existed within you.

His eyes stare down at you in contempt as he booms,

"You don't belong here—you're far away from home here—there's nothing here for you.

From down the end of the bar, another voice looms out of the internal fog.

"My child...come to me."

What peace...what certainty...what authority you find in this voice!

"Come to me, my child."

Once again, more silently than the first, but irresistibly compelling, you walk as though mesmerized toward this man.

You are drawn to his peace.

He seems a pillar of security, and an island of calm in the midst of chaos.

You reach for his hand and feel the breadth and depth of his gentle strength.

His full beard is as white as snow with kindly eyes seeing only the good.

He lifts you to his lap and says,

"Do not be afraid. I am with you always."

You are captivated by his eyes which appear as orbs of silent wisdom and empathy as old as time itself. He says,

"I have a gift for you—something to remember me by."

From his pocket, he produces a gleaming white marble.

It glows brilliant and dazzling in the darkness of the turmoil inside this place.

It shines as though polished with light from another world. He holds it with the tips of his fingers and places it so gracefully and incredulously in the center of your brain, as he explains,

"This white marble is my power in your brain. Its eternal logic bestows only thoughts of the true reality...no longer do you invest in illusions...no longer do you distort your world with thoughts of fantasy.

The power of this radiant sphere brings you the truth of right thinking.

Whenever you are confused, remember the white marble at the very center of your brain— unceasingly emitting celestial light and heavenly warmth, and crowding out the darkness of fear with the healing light of peace. "

Thoughts
Guided Healing Imagery 2

Imagine a small, white, round marble embedded in the center of your brain. This marble is the receptor site for all of God's healing power/grace from your thinking spiritual strength (Faith, Wisdom, Steadfastness, Wholeness, or Charity). You notice that the white marble is very tarnished, dirty, blemished, dull, and generally covered in a rust-like corrosion that completely blocks out God's healing power/grace from getting through.

To remedy the situation, you decide to descend to the fountain of healing water in your soul. Your soul is deep within you and can only be accessed by a long spiral stairway.

NOTE: Proceed with the healing-guided imagery found on page 39.

Thinking Prayer

Open my Mind, Lord

Dearest Lord, let me always remember that your healing power is in my mind. This power is the central healing force in the universe. I have your permission; indeed I have your instruction, to seize it because it is my inheritance.

My doubts are meaningless in the surety and certainty of your Love.

Let me remember that it is your Will alone that makes me happy. Now, let there be silence in my mind. I seek no further for I have found my goal. There is no other.

I have come to where the road is carpeted with goodness and truth, fallen from trees of mercy and forgiveness.

They are now underfoot, and as I look up to heaven I recognize peace at last and feel its soft embrace surround my heart and mind with comfort and with love.

Let my mind rest in the Holy Spirit who offers me single freedom. Let me be free and carry freedom as my gift to those who still believe they are enslaved within their body.

The darkness of the night of my thoughts is over now; I can come to the light together with you.

Let me come daily to this holy place inside to spend some time together and share my dream of unity long forgotten but now remembered.

Amen

Chapter Six
Feeling, Depression, and Illness

Directions

The following page contains a "Feeling Function Continuum." As truthfully and accurately as possible, circle the number on the 1-10 number line that best indicates how and what you believe about yourself at this general time in your life.

Responses 1-5 indicate relative agreement with the descriptor on the left side of the number line, while responses 6-10 indicate progressively greater agreement with the descriptor on the right side. Add up all 10 of your responses and place your total score at the bottom of the page in the space provided. This score is a very rough approximation of the level of your feeling function mood right now.

Please NOTE: A clinical diagnosis of depression can only be made by a trained mental health professional.

Feeling Function Continuum

I feel mostly glum								I feel light and bright.	
1	2	3	4	5	6	7	8	9	10

I feel despair in my heart.								I feel joy in my heart.	
1	2	3	4	5	6	7	8	9	10

I feel barren and stark.								I feel blooming and verdant.	
1	2	3	4	5	6	7	8	9	10

I feel forlorn and heavy-hearted.						I feel enthusiastic/light-hearted.			
1	2	3	4	5	6	7	8	9	10

I feel vulnerable and unprotected.						I feel safe, secure, and stable.			
1	2	3	4	5	6	7	8	9	10

I feel guilty.									I feel special.
1	2	3	4	5	6	7	8	9	10

I worry a lot.								I am free of worry.	
1	2	3	4	5	6	7	8	9	10

I feel inadequate/unsuccessful.							I feel a sense of vitality.		
1	2	3	4	5	6	7	8	9	10

I have a very somber mood.						I have a very effervescent mood.			
1	2	3	4	5	6	7	8	9	10

I feel a significant loss of hope.								I have lots of hope.	
1	2	3	4	5	6	7	8	9	10

My total "feeling" affect score is _____.

You can now go to page 115 and transfer this total score onto the respective number line you see there.

Love and Fear

All feelings flow from only two primal sources: love and fear. The so-called **enabling feelings** like confidence, inner strength, joy, ecstasy, and the like all flow from the wellspring of Love. All **paralyzing feelings** like confusion, depression, anxiety, sadness, frustration and the like all flow from the absence of Love...fear! It's been said that the happiest people are those who have mastered the skill of extinguishing their paralyzing feelings and extending their enabling ones. This skill becomes crucial as you proceed along your illness journey.

Illness can contort your feelings and push you into many paralyzing feelings like hate, fear, and anger. At some deep place, you hate that things have to be this way; you're afraid they will only get worse; and you're angry that no one seems capable of helping. Somehow you know in your heart that while the darkness that grips your emotions seems very real, it is but a deception.

It's only fear that stops you from fully embracing God's divine guidance.

At some even deeper place, perhaps unconscious place, you know that the hate, fear and anger merely cover up an underlying and essential loneliness, that of feeling all alone. This loneliness violates some internal contract that says someone should be there to pull you out of this mess. But this deception makes you feel even more fearful that your deception may be found out. So you work hard and exert tremendous energy to establish the reality, the justification for hanging onto your hate, fear, and anger. You find scapegoats for your illness—you may blame your doctors, you may blame yourself, or sometimes you blame others around you. All too often a favorite target for blame is God.

You sometimes feel lost, in your heart of hearts you feel like an orphan now—abandoned for no apparent purpose, destined only to feel pain and suffering. From time to time however you feel something very different...a soft touch of home within you that pulls you like a magnet to your **true spiritual home**. You can make a hundred homes here and yet not settle your feelings of restlessness for something else. There is a child within you who feels an alien here and who simply wants to go home.

Sigmund Freud once remarked that he thought all of his therapy patients felt like aliens and simply wanted to go home. Unfortunately he surmised that the home we seek is our mother's womb. He had a good idea; he just had the wrong place. Perhaps we all do want to go home; this is certainly true when we feel the fearsome pangs of depression and the "attacks" of illness. No, we don't want to die to go home, but we do seek the warm security of a place where we are at peace and feel whole, safe, and happy. This seems a simple request.

Depression may be asking you to surrender your heart to God's healing care.

Emotional pain may be a signal that an unforgiveness lies deep in your mind. Release the pain by reframing the thought that produced the terrifying feeling. God does not will that you suffer; God only wills that you find the truth. God helps you forgive the thousand and one faults over which you blame and discredit yourself. Humility does not mean self-condemnation or self-denial...it simply means finding and embracing the truth. Each time you feel the stab of pain caused by paralyzing emotions, realize that you are holding the knife. This weapon is but the **thoughts of condemnation** you infuse into your mind as you forget that you are a child of God. You need to shift your thinking to release yourself from such paralyzing feelings.

How can you fully accept your illness, anger, and depression rather than moving to fear as a false protection? When you see them as your enemies and fight against them, you only ensure that they remain with you. The two emotions that keep things close to you are love and hate, and hate is a secondary emotion to fear. You certainly don't want to love your illness, anger, or depression, but you might hate them.

When you fight illness and depression, they can become stronger and leave you depleted. On the other hand, when you accept illness and depression without attacking them, you remain strong to do **the healing work you are called to do**. When you attack, you are always sad and left either angry and/or depressed; and when you are helpless, you are also sad and likewise left either angry or depressed.

The Middle Way

What is needed is the strong middle way...the way defined by the desert philosophers and echoed by the great thinkers of the Middle Ages that is best summarized in the Latin *in medio stat virtus* (in the middle stands the strength). This is the philosophy of the Spiritual Strengths Healing Plan...the middle way. Entrust your diagnosis, and all the illness that oozes from it, to God and you will feel your innate strength return to you.

The losses of illness admixed with depression may be the fire, sometimes the painful fire, that sears away all that blocks your healing.

At the deepest part of you is your **singular holiness**—that silent and sacred place where pain is no longer, where all sorrow ends, and where all problems are solved. You are holy because your true reality comes from God. Your holiness makes you whole and makes no demands. Your world self sees you as separate from God and therefore incomplete; it only sees demands. Demands produce a feeling of deficit, restlessness, and indecision. You are strong when you can see past what things appear to be, and you keep a steady gaze upon the light of your spiritual strengths within you.

The Child Within

There's a three-year old child within you who seeks to be reunited with the sweetness of home that he remembers only faintly. The child is defenseless, and yet the apostle Paul reminds us that it in our weakness (defenselessness) is where we find our strength. In the language of spiritual strengths, this means that it's in your shadows and your compulsions where you find your spiritual strengths, because you couldn't feel the sour sting of your shadows and compulsions if you didn't first have the spiritual strength. You could not genuinely and comprehensively experience the spiritual strength of hope, for example, if you hadn't tasted, even a little bit, the sourness of hope's shadow of despair, and/or the emptiness of hope's compulsion of presumption.

Divine healing action requires a heart inclined to the light within.

Nonetheless, in the vulnerable posture of illness, only intensified by depression, you can feel like an alien here and very much want to go home. Yet this child is like an angel who speaks to you of home and beckons you to find rest. This child speaks not as a vulnerable, dependent, and fearful weakling, but almost as **a prophetic voice of hope.** You are to listen to your inner child— nurturing and nourishing—because your inner child will bring you peaceful respite from the tumult of illness that is only amplified by anger and depression.

Depression as a 3-4 Rut

Another way to see depression is as a 3-4 rut. The "3" refers to the thinking function of your personality, and the "4" is your feeling function. According to highly regarded "cognitive therapy," the thoughts you put in your mind (which you most certainly do put in there) have direct and immediate impact on your feelings. The thoughts you create in your "thinking function" (#3) produce the feelings in your "feeling function" (#4)! When and if you create a succession of negative thoughts, you consequently generate a succession of negative feelings.

My clinical experience tells me that if this process of negative thinking becomes a repeated and common experience, that puts you at risk of falling into what I call a 3—4 rut, where instead of proceeding to the "deciding function" (#5) of your personality after experiencing a feeling (#4), which is normal and healthy, you instead swing back to your "thinking function" (#3) with another negative thought, which in turn generates another negative feeling, which is diverted back to the thinking function again where it generates another negative thought...and the negative spiral, or rut continues. Let me give you a personal example...

Let's say that after teaching a class where I think that I was not at my best, I give myself a thought such as—

Initial thought: *"I didn't perform very well today in class."*

  ↓   ↓   ↓

This thought generates a feeling of <u>disappointment</u>.

  ↓   ↓   ↓

Instead of going to the deciding function **where I could**

formulate a plan to do better the next time, I swing back to my thinking function and generate a new thought…

↓   ↓   ↓

"Come to think of it, the same thing happened last week in class."

↓   ↓   ↓

Such a thought only intensifies my feeling of disappointment…I now feel <u>depleted</u>.

↓   ↓   ↓

Again I divert my personality away from making a decision and swing back to my thinking function again, where I think…

↓   ↓   ↓

"I think I'm losing my effectiveness as a teacher."

↓   ↓   ↓

This thought only intensifies my depleted feeling and produces a feeling of <u>discouragement</u>.

↓   ↓   ↓

And again I swing to my thinking function, and think…

↓   ↓   ↓

"I'm not a very good teacher."

↓   ↓   ↓

This thought produces a <u>sad</u> feeling in me which leads me to think something like…

↓   ↓   ↓

I shouldn't have become a teacher."

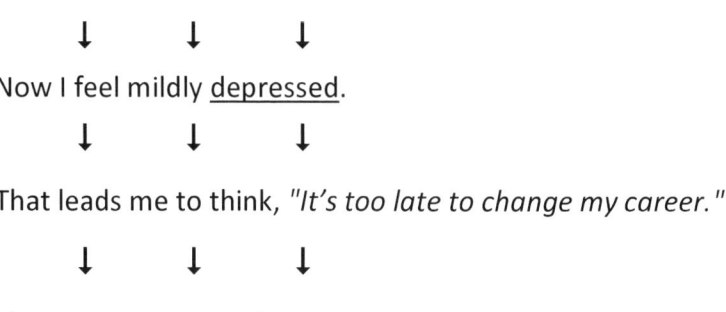

↓   ↓   ↓

Now I feel mildly <u>depressed</u>.

↓   ↓   ↓

That leads me to think, *"It's too late to change my career."*

↓   ↓   ↓

That in turn leads to feelings of being <u>trapped, helpless,</u> <u>and more depressed</u>.

↓   ↓   ↓

My new thought after that becomes, *"I'm pretty much a failure!"*

↓   ↓   ↓

This, of course, leads me to feel <u>very depressed</u>!

I think you can see the viciousness of the 3—4 rut if it is left unattended. It can rob your personality of flexibility and creativity and make you negative and ineffective; it can intensify feelings of helplessness, consequently diminish your internal resilience, and undercut the power and might of God's power/grace in you...your six spiritual strengths.

Simple Relaxation Sequence Procedure

Before you move on to the following guided-imagery sequences, you'll want to prepare your mind, heart, and soul by going through the simple relaxation sequence procedure described on page 38.

Feelings

Guided Healing Imagery 1

You are six years old.

It's winter...sleet falls and stings your cheeks as you walk down a street of shadows.

You're in a "bad" neighborhood in a large city that is full of trash.

You feel glances of anger out the windows.

A hollow and sunken feeling invades your very core.

Your heart is heavy and races with fear.

You're lonely...all alone in this strange, cold, and fearsome place.

This is not your home.

You feel confused...what should you do?

You're lost...can you trust to ask for help?

You begin to feel not only afraid, but now a hate arises in your heart.

Hate for the situation you face...unknowing how it came to be, and hate that no one can seem to help.

Suddenly you spy a light, a faint glow of a single candle shining through a stained glass window.

You run to it, open the large oak door, and walk out of the sleet and cold and wind. You walk out of the hollow fear and uncertainty...

And find your home.

Your home is a church, empty now...such peace...candles burning...sweet incense...warmth...stillness...retreat...

Kneeling in the front pew, you bow your head.

A sweet presence of peace overtakes you. Opening your arms, you raise your face to the cross.

A beam of white light slowly forms and shines forth from the intersection of the cross and makes its way to you.

It strikes your breast with soothing warmth and penetrates to your heart where it places a white marble of blazing light.

This marble seems to magnify the light beam and reflect it out in every direction from your heart.

The marble seems to extend the beautiful sparkle of the energy-beam, increasing its splendor and intensifying its luminescence.

Gradually, a gentle and welcome peace overtakes your heart...calm and confidence enters in and pervades your affective world.

Listening, you hear, "You are my child in whom I am well pleased—go out and extend my love. Be joyful as you find life in abundance, and remember I am with you always."

Your heart fills with inner strength, joy, and even spiritual ecstasy.

A place of inner holiness has been made for you...a place where only hope and faith can enter, and from this place the celestial energy emanates outward entering every place of darkness in your being and cleansing away all sadness, sorrow, frustration, anger, and depression.

You are now free.

Out of the church now you return to the city street. Although it's the same street, it has been transformed.

No fear—only love…no ugliness…only beauty.

No distrust—only truth…nothing bad…only goodness.

The white marble in your heart beams out a brilliant light of power and glory, which illuminates your formerly dismal world and makes it new…thereby making you new, too.

Whenever sadness or anger threatens…remember the white marble in your heart.

It is ever-present, continuously pumping cosmic light, extending God's peace and tranquility throughout your world. Never will you be alone again…the white marble remains in your heart.

Feelings

Guided Healing Imagery 2

Imagine a small white round marble embedded in the center of your heart. This marble is the receptor site for all of God's healing power/grace from your feeling spiritual strength (either Joy, Trust, Love-Finder, Empathy or Gratitude). You notice that the white marble is very tarnished, dirty, blemished, dull, and generally covered in a rust-like corrosion that completely blocks out God's healing power/grace from getting through.

To remedy the situation, you decide to descend to the fountain of healing water in your soul. Your soul is deep within you accessed only by a long spiral stairway.

NOTE: Proceed with the healing-guided imagery you found on page 39.

NOTE: Proceed with the healing-guided imagery you found on page 39.

Feeling Prayer

Come in my Heart, Lord

Let me be still a moment and go home, for I feel an alien here outside the barely perceptible yet so supportive feeling of sweetness I remember...sometimes not more than a tiny throb deep inside me.

Lord God, help me lay down my weapons of fear, anger, and hate and instead find rest—listening to my child within who would take me home.

My spiritual strengths see through divine eyes; they do not feel the small, the weak, the sickly and the dying, the helpless and afraid, the poor, the sad, the starving and the joyless in me.

My strengths feel only the opposite of these as part of your abundance of joyful membership in your family.

I am at home only in you, dear Lord; my status is not as an alien but simply as your natural holy child.

I cherish my home and the healing balm of your love warming my heart and penetrating my soul.

I rest untroubled, sure that only good can come to me.

The stillness of my soul remains untouched and undisturbed by the shrill, strident, and frantic assaults of illness and depression, which I now realize were futile efforts of the world to wrestle me from my middle center in you.

Amen

Chapter Seven
Deciding, Depression, and Illness

Directions

The following page contains a "Deciding Function Continuum." As truthfully and accurately as possible, circle the number on the 1-10 number line that best indicates how and what you believe about yourself at this general time in your life.

Responses 1-5 indicate relative agreement with the descriptor on the left side of the number line, while responses 6-10 indicate progressively greater agreement with the descriptor on the right side. Add up all 10 of your responses and place your total score at the bottom of the page in the space provided. This score is a very rough approximation of the level of your deciding function mood right now.

Please NOTE: A clinical diagnosis of depression can only be made by a trained mental health professional.

Deciding Function Continuum

I just want to give up.								I carry on with steadfastness
1	2	3	4	5	6	7	8	9	10

I deny myself pleasures.								I am kind to myself.
1	2	3	4	5	6	7	8	9	10

It's difficult to make decisions.								It's easy to make decisions.
1	2	3	4	5	6	7	8	9	10

I can't stick to plans/objectives.								I have resolve.
1	2	3	4	5	6	7	8	9	10

I blame myself.								I easily forgive myself.
1	2	3	4	5	6	7	8	9	10

I am rarely satisfied.								I am grateful and appreciative.
1	2	3	4	5	6	7	8	9	10

It is hard to organize priorities.								I have clear priorities.
1	2	3	4	5	6	7	8	9	10

I choose what is negative.								I choose positive paths.
1	2	3	4	5	6	7	8	9	10

I can't formulate strategies.								I develop constructive strategies.
1	2	3	4	5	6	7	8	9	10

It is hard to stick to my decisions.								I am resolute in my decisions.
1	2	3	4	5	6	7	8	9	10

My total "deciding" affect score is _____.

You can now go to page 115 and transfer this total score onto the respective number line you see there.

The Decisions Imperative

You cannot direct your life, or even co-direct your life along with God, without making decisions. Not making a decision is actually making one. You cannot stand still; you must change. This developmental **imperative of change** and growth is the reason you need decisions, and you need to make them constantly. Without decisions you cannot grow; without decisions you cannot heal.

Depression may let you turn your shadows and compulsions to your ultimate advantage.

Every one of your decisions is always a choice, some of which you are aware, and some not. You make the choices from among a series of options. These options are based upon your priorities, goals, and objectives, which are previous decisions you have made, either consciously or not. You also decide the strategies you will employ to achieve these goals. True decisions represent your most honest preferences...what you want. Decisions convert dreams and possibilities into potential actions. Decisions are like headlights on your car on a dark night—without them you can't go very far safely.

Feelings and Decisions

You cannot make accurate and healing-generating decisions without first dealing healthfully with your feelings. You can mishandle your feelings by—

1. Stuffing them inside you.

2. Resisting, fighting, or denying them.

3. Projecting them onto another situation or person.

4. Disguising them as thoughts or as another "acceptable" but fraudulent feeling.

To counter these feelings "tricks" of ill-health, you need to—

1. Express your feeling clearly, directly, and healthfully.

2. Consciously decide to do nothing.

3. Allow your feelings to wash over you.

4. Diffuse your feelings by changing the thoughts that generated them in the first place.

Free Will

Who is in charge of your free will? Can you imagine what your free will looks like? If your free will were a person, what would she/he look like? Can you picture this in your mind's eye?

Depression may paradoxically help you abandon your false self and embrace God's healing abundance...your True Self.

The central question and decision of your illness journey, and indeed at all times of your life, is, "*Do you want to be right or do you want to be happy?*" If your answer is to be happy, then here are the rules for decision-making:

1. Everything has a purpose. You need to continuously choose to communicate to yourself that your illness, indeed everything that has happened in your life and will happen, occurs for a purpose, but that most times you are blind to that purpose.

2. Make no decisions by yourself. God is always your co-decision maker; consult God in every decision you make.

3. Decide what kind of a day you want and prepare for it to be given to you. Periodically remind yourself throughout the day what kind of a day you would like.
4. Try to give the decision to the Holy Spirit. When and if you feel uneasy, remember that without ever knowing it, you have made a decision by yourself on your own terms.
5. If you can't give the decision to the Holy Spirit, then you can begin to change your mind with this statement, *"At least I can decide that I do not like what I feel right now."*
6. Then ask, *"What is another way I could look at this?*

The Simple Choice

All the seemingly innumerable distinctions of choice, and all the possibilities that seem almost endless, all boil down to one simple decision (which can be asked in a number of ways): *"Do I choose love or do I chose fear? Do I choose life or do I choose death? Do I choose God's view or do I choose the world's view?* All of these are the same decision. Decide today to take your rightful place as the collaborator with God in running your life. Your surrender to God (which is always an intentional decision) is your constant choice. The power of decision is your own. In a sense, **this world is a great classroom** where you are continuously challenged to make the right choice.

Always choose Love. Whatever your eventual action…always choose in Love. Let's take a look at an example from my counseling files. A man confronts his wife with the statement, *"You didn't put out my tennis shorts, and you put out the short summer socks instead of my longer, winter socks!"* What is his wife to do? How can she choose in Love? She has choices…

- Choice one: *"Yes, of course I'll fix it right away."*

- Choice two: *"You know, I feel rather discounted when you treat me like the maid."*

- Choice three: *"In love I want to tell you that I'd rather you picked out your own clothes in the future."*

Which response would be the best? Where did each of these potential responses come from: spiritual strengths, shadows, or compulsions?

Depression may help you to decide to give over all to God...to empty yourself so healing can flood in.

Become keenly aware of the many, many decisions you have in front of you every day. You have decisions even down to the very thoughts and feelings you choose to give yourself. Each time you recognize that a decision is required, turn first to call upon the name of God in prayer. Listen to the voice within. Words are insignificant when a child of God calls upon his parent's name. Try to make God's thought your own. Naturally you can only approach this crudely, but perhaps the most accurate means you have is to "fly" to your spiritual strengths, because God's voice resides there.

You have been given the power of decision, of free will, as a means to letting go of illusions (shadows and compulsions). Deciding to forgive is the means by which your ultimate fear, the fear of death, is overcome. Perhaps you need to forgive yourself for believing the illusion that at some psychic level, you mistook your body for your Real Self. To that degree you believed in the world rather than in God—you invested in fear rather than in Love.

Depression pulls you apart so you can let God rearrange the pieces into a single whole and receive healing.

You can make the decision to change an attitude by deciding to change your way of thinking on a certain subject. Think a new thought over and over again and you will transform it into an attitude and in so doing transform your personality functioning. Healing requires that you decide to look upon everything with Love. Your expressions of Love are your means to find healing. Healing always involves letting go; when you give Love you receive it, and when you let go of fear, you free yourself to express Love.

Simple Relaxation Sequence Procedure...

Before you move on to the two following guided imagery sequences, you'll want to prepare your mind, heart, and soul by going through the simple relaxation sequence procedure described on page 38.

Decisions

Guided Healing Imagery 1

You are your present age and literally see yourself hacking your way through a dense jungle with a machete.

It's a dark and foreboding swamp with snakes and other scary "critters."

With humidity dripping from every leaf, it sounds just like a thunderstorm.

Minutes turn into hours, and finally night falls.

You spend the night in a tree...moss covered...spiders and ants tirelessly crawl about.

With no food...you begin again in the morning.

By midday, you're exhausted, fatigued, emotionally at the end of your rope.

You finally see a clearing up ahead.

You see a long swaying suspension bridge made of vines over a 1000 foot chasm with a wild river below.

Panicked by heights...the thought of crossing that bridge is just too frightening.

Yet there is no other way.

You make the conscious choice to step out in faith.

Inching out, you finally get about one-third out when you glance down for the first time only to freeze.

You cannot move...you are literally frozen in fear.

Tears well up and roll down your face...you're unable to move.

You decide to pray..."Dearest Lord, give me the power to move on."

You hear and feel nothing.

"Father, be with me now in my time of need, give me strength, infuse my will with your will."

Upon finishing this prayer, you miraculously feel the warmth of a body next to yours...steadying you with a strong arm around your waist.

The most comforting voice you ever heard says, "Do not be afraid. I am with you always...

I have given you my light in your soul so you can believe...

I have given you my light in your eyes so you can see...

I have given you my light in your mind so you can think thoughts of wholeness, and...

I have given you my light in your heart so you can feel peace and love.

Now, I place the white marble of my truth in your gut so you can choose to do my will."

You realize now that you must go forward...

All that seemed to paralyze you has evaporated away...you now feel free to progress.

Your fear is still with you, but it no longer cripples you—the light of truth, beauty, and goodness fills your will and overpowers the darkness of fear. Your will, located in the deepest part of your gut, is infused with brilliance and the luster of the eternal now.

Your will now glows with the power of the cosmos because it's now aligned with the will of God.

You are a child of God and you have now received your inheritance.

Your will, now in concert with God's will, shines with a beauty so grand that you hardly recognize it as you.

You are the transformed person—you no longer need to resist or fight a fraudulent will that is aligned with the world—for you are now in keeping with Love.

You step out onto the bridge and walk erect and strong, albeit slowly, knowing you are not alone.

Reaching the other side, you feel the arm around your waist loosen and fall away.

You feel this small loss, but you are not lonely—your will continues to shine with a transformed light.

You walk a bit down a path and confront a fork in the path. Which way to go? Which path to take?

A pang of doubt emerges in you for but an instant before your white marble of truth and choice bursts into a glorious bonanza of light—a show beyond your imagination.

Now you are ready to choose.

You decide to take the path that seems most risky because you know that this path offers you the most growth in God's world.

Every time you make a decision, you consult the white marble of choice and ask, "What would God do in this situation? What does God expect of me?"

You choose the risky path and find a field of flowers so beautiful, so right, so good...and you carry the fragrance of these heavenly flowers with you all day.

Decisions

Guided Healing Imagery 2

Imagine a small white round marble embedded in the center of your gut, just below your belly button. This marble is the receptor site for all of God's healing power/grace from your deciding spiritual strength (either Harmony, Patience, Strength, Transcendence, or Self-Discipline). You notice that the white marble is very tarnished, dirty, blemished, dull, and generally covered in a rust-like corrosion that completely blocks-out God's healing power/grace from getting through.

To remedy the situation you decide to descend to the fountain of healing water in your soul. Your soul is deep within you accessed only by a long spiral stairway.

NOTE: Proceed with the healing guided imagery as you found on page 39.

Deciding Prayer
Guide my Decisions, Lord

Dear Lord, today let me truly know and understand that the power of decision is mine.

I know that it is your will that I accept myself fully as what you created me to be.

Let me be humble in acknowledging my inheritance of mightiness.

Each time I am tempted to be angry is actually my opportunity to find freedom—as I decide to choose love instead of fear.

When I forgive those who I thought trespassed against me, I see that they are actually one with me.

Lord, I seek release from the chains that bind me to this world. Let me devote today to my search in profound solitude so I may find you and join with you to make my decisions your decisions.

You have given me so many gifts; let me honor your gift of free will so I can make decisions of conscious intent about my illness.

Let me take your hand, Lord, and walk with you today and allow me to make my will your will.

Let me practice daily knowing that faith develops from practice and truth comes from understanding the meaning you give to my life.

Amen

Chapter Eight
Acting, Depression, and Illness

Directions

The following page contains a "Acting Function Continuum." As truthfully and accurately as possible, circle the number on the 1-10 number line that best indicates how and what you believe about yourself at this general time in your life.

Responses 1-5 indicate relative agreement with the descriptor on the left side of the number line, while responses 6-10 indicate progressively greater agreement with the descriptor on the right side. Add up all 10 of your responses and place your total score at the bottom of the page in the space provided. This score is a very rough approximation of the level of your acting function mood right now.

Please NOTE: A clinical diagnosis of depression can only be made by a trained mental health professional.

Acting Function Continuum

I cannot let go of the negative.								I can let go of the negative.	
1	2	3	4	5	6	7	8	9	10

I can't participate in pleasures.							I can participate in feeling good.		
1	2	3	4	5	6	7	8	9	10

I act as though I'm grief-stricken.						I act like I just heard great news.			
1	2	3	4	5	6	7	8	9	10

I act like I am weighed down.						I am graceful and deliberate.			
1	2	3	4	5	6	7	8	9	10

I act against myself.						I act in my own best interest.			
1	2	3	4	5	6	7	8	9	10

I lack focused purpose.						I exercise singleness of purpose.			
1	2	3	4	5	6	7	8	9	10

I am usually distracted.						I am usually quite focused.			
1	2	3	4	5	6	7	8	9	10

I tend to brood.							I am free of remorse.		
1	2	3	4	5	6	7	8	9	10

I persist in blaming myself.						I very rarely blame myself.			
1	2	3	4	5	6	7	8	9	10

I act with little success.							I act in successful ways.		
1	2	3	4	5	6	7	8	9	10

My total "acting" affect score is _____.

You can now go to page 115 and transfer this total score onto the respective number line you see there.

You Need Action

You need more than the first five functions of your personality to find the means to overcome the angst of anger and the demon of depression that may flow from your illness. Your sixth personality function is imperative...you need action. God is a God of action, and it is action that initiates every great success. Action is what produces results. Healing requires that you learn how to take effective action with both illness and depression.

Action has been defined as a cause set in motion. To have a cause, you must make a decision. If you wish to be holy (whole and centered in your personality), if you wish to engage and be led by your spirit self, then you must change your physical and mental actions to match the state of your spiritual journey with illness.

Divine healing action responds to your spiritual strengths which can open the flood gates of your soul and allow the universal flow of love/healing to wash over you—cleansing you and bringing you to peace.

What are the actions that can set your healing cause in motion? What are the actions that can bring you spiritual wholeness...to enter God's house and find peace? **"Right" action requires that you unburden yourself** of all that you kept from God and give it over to the packet of divinity at your center. God alone knows the secrets of healing and the way to peace. Each and every day of your illness journey, make sure you spend time with God and try always to offer forgiveness everywhere. God will take the final steps toward healing for you, but in preparation you must take a thousand tiny steps toward God.

Forgiveness and Acceptance

Forgiveness is a premier healing action; it is the bridge you walk over to happiness. Offer thanks to God because in God all things will eventually find their ultimate freedom. It's in forgiveness, animated by your spiritual strengths, where the pain of your illness will find healing. Judgment will always bring pain, and attack will always boomerang back and slice you. Attack, in any form, will bring you distress. The thought you can somehow enhance yourself through self-seeking will only nail you to your own cross. Forgiveness is essential for you to perform your function today.

Beyond forgiveness, a second action necessary for healing is acceptance. What exactly are you called to accept? You are a child of God, not of the world. You are not only a body, but also a mind and spirit. Love is your only cause today. Acceptance is also essential for you to perform your function of healing today.

Depression may be the dark night of your soul...a time when the seeds of your spiritual strengths take root in your soul, eventually allowing them to grow into colorful flowers of beauty and towering trees of strength.

Love Actions

How do you discern to what degree your actions are loving actions? Here are some questions that might help you discern...

1. Is this action in keeping with God's will as you understand it?

2. Does this action honor those around you, especially those directly or indirectly affected by your action?

3. Is this action meeting your real, essential needs, or is it pandering to your optional wants or the wants of others?

4. Does this action allow you increased honesty, wholeness, and peace?

5. What is the basic lesson of the action?

6. Is this action consistent with your values, attitudes, and beliefs?

7. Does this action honor your family?

8. Is this action virtuous?

9. Does this action accept reality or distort it?

10. Is this action the result of your deliberate, conscious, and enlightened process of discernment?

Simple Relaxation Sequence Procedure...

Before you move on to the following guided-imagery sequences, you'll want to prepare your mind, heart, and soul by going through the simple relaxation sequence procedure described on page 38.

Actions
Guided Healing Imagery 1

God reminds us that, "In my house there are many mansions." These mansions are magnificent spiritual dwelling places that we construct with our own hands. These are edifices of love we build bit by bit through our love-actions.

Imagine your love mansion in heaven.

Actually picture and visualize the most beautiful spiritual mansion you can.

In your mind's eye, see the gate and the celestial road that leads up to it.

Stand from afar now and view the entire spiritual indwelling.

Look at the beautiful grounds...the gorgeous structure...the verdant gardens...the heavenly foliage...the reflecting pools.

Imagine the materials used to construct your mansion.

These are not earthly materials but celestial ones.

These are the same materials that made the city of God.

Your mansion glows in luminescence...it glistens in the heavenly light that seems to envelope it.

God teaches you to lay up treasures in God's house, not here in your earthly house in this world.

God's world is made of Love...its building blocks are acts of love.

You can construct your heavenly mansion while you're here on this earth.

Imagine and visualize that each and every time you complete an act of love you assemble another small bit of your heavenly abode.

You actually build your heaven while you're here on this earth.

This is your true reality of love.

Love is your medium of exchange...it's your coin of the realm.

Love is all...everywhere...everything.

Each time you exercise and extend love through actions of mercy, or loyalty, or faithfulness, you build your heavenly mansion to an even more magnificent level of grandeur.

The actual and the symbolic parts of your body that perform action are your hands, your feet, and your tongue.

Hold the white marble of peace in your hand.

Visualize it empowering your hands to perform the mightiest task of the universe...loving.

Feel the power as it flows from the marble of strength into your hands and up your arms and throughout your entire body— endowing it with a heavenly energy not found anywhere in this world.

This is the force of love which is all powerful...omnipotent...the force that holds sway in the universe.

This is the love power you have in you so you can act well...you can act in healing.

Imagine your marble of majesty embedded in the palms of both your hands, both your feet, and on your tongue.

Imagine them permanently there giving you the special gift of God's love potency everywhere you go.

Offer love and you extend God's domain—thereby building up the city of God here on this earth.

Offer love and arm yourself with the strength and the authority of the cosmos.

Teach love in your action and everything will be given to you.

Imagine the brilliant rays of love light extending from your palms, your feet, and your tongue outward in every direction—spreading the true reality...the ultimate power of God into the world.

You are God's emissary here in your little corner of the world.

Your actions of love are God's actions.

Your forgiveness is God's love in action.

Your kindness...your acceptance...your self-control...your happiness...your delight...your joy...all of this and so much more is God's love in action.

God has invested in you; God's beams of heavenly light are with you today as you make your appointed rounds on this earth.

God's white marbles of love-power are in your soul so that you might believe in love; are in your eyes that you might continuously see love; are in your mind that you might always think love; are in your heart that you might feel love; are in your gut so you might choose love; and are in your hands, feet, and tongue so you might act in love.

Actions

Guided Healing Imagery 2

Imagine a small white marble embedded in the center of your hands, your feet, and on your tongue. These marbles are the receptor sites for all of God's healing power/grace from your acting spiritual strength (either Truth, Inspiration, Kindness, Courage, or Perseverance). You notice that the white marbles are very tarnished, dirty, blemished, dull, and generally covered in a rust-like corrosion that completely blocks out God's healing power/grace from getting through.

To remedy the situation, you decide to descend to the fountain of healing water in your soul. Your soul is deep within you accessed only by a long spiral stairway.

NOTE: Proceed with the healing-guided imagery as you found on page 39.

Acting Prayer
Guide my Decisions, Lord

Lord, I know my feet have reached the beautiful lawns that begin the grounds to heaven's gate.

Let me pass all anxiety, depression, and guilt.

Let me accept and release the world from my false expectations.

Allow me to take the action of letting go of the future—I know it is in your hands; I have no control over it except to express my powerlessness.

As I escape all fear of future pain, I find my way to present peace and certainty the world cannot provide nor can it threaten.

Let me hear the song of heaven and the voice of the Spirit as I release the world from any expectations that I had of it.

This world provides me with no safety; on the contrary it seems rooted in attack, all its "gifts" are but deceptions.

Help me, dear Lord, to release my defensiveness and align my true self with your defenselessness.

Loose me from the iron grip that attack has upon my heart. Lord, give me courage and strength to act as you would have me act— in love and in peace—with your Spirit as my model and guide.

As of this moment, I give my life to you, dear Lord, forever.

Amen

Postscript

This book is a journey, a healing journey to your very center. Along the way you've discovered that you may have unconsciously adopted anger and/or depression in a vain and illusionary attempt to protect yourself from further loss and pain. Yet, you've also discovered that anger and depression, the very tools you've blindly chosen to help you, are but weapons that can damage your soul.

In these pages you've discovered how to escape from the web of anger and depression, and that it's only by adopting "the middle way" of your spiritual strengths that true healing is found. It is only in embracing your shadows and compulsions that true healing can begin.

Your spiritual strengths will always prevail over your shadows and compulsions. The "fallout" from the battle between and among your spiritual strengths, shadows, and compulsions is anger and depression. Anger and depression are actually results of your fear that the shadows and compulsions might just win the battle and leave you alone and destitute. This can never happen.

You are a child of God and your inheritance of Love ensures that you are safe and secure in that Love. Strive to always be "in your middle," strive to place your spiritual strengths as your "True North." Dedicate each day to one of your spiritual strengths...look for it each day...seek and you will find. This is the path to real healing.

Appendix I

Transfer your scores from the respective chapters. Add your six scores and divide by 6 to generate your total mood score. This score is a very rough approximation of the level of your overall mood right now.

Note: A clinical diagnosis of depression can only be made by a trained mental health professional.

Believing Function (page 32)
10   20   30   40   50   60   70   80   90   100

Perceiving Function (page 46)
10   20   30   40   50   60   70   80   90   100

Thinking Function (page 62)
10   20   30   40   50   60   70   80   90   100

Feeling Function (page 76)
10   20   30   40   50   60   70   80   90   100

Deciding Function (page 90)
10   20   30   40   50   60   70   80   90   100

Acting Function (page 104)
10   20   30   40   50   60   70   80   90   100

Totals from all six _____ Divided by 6 = _____ (your total mood score)

Made in the USA
Charleston, SC
06 November 2015